Greetings From Florida

ALABAMA

SAN FRANCISCO

Greetings from BOSTON

GREETINGS FROM Baltimore MD

GREETINGS FROM MAINE

GREETINGS FROM
CALIFORNIA
PLAYGROUND OF THE NATION
PORTLAND
OREGON
Greetings
from the
Aloha State
-Hawaii
WELCOME
TO
OKLAHOMA
UTAH
GREETINGS FROM
TEXAS
TEXAS STATE FLAG
TEXAS LONGHORN
Greetings
from
MINNESOTA
Greetings
From
NORTH DAKOTA
Greetings from KANSAS
Greetings
from
NEW
JERSEY
THE GARDEN STATE
GREETINGS FROM
MAINE
Greetings
from
NEW ORLEANS
LOUISIANA
SAN
FRANCISCO
Greetings From
Florida
GREETINGS FROM
ATLANTA
Georgia
GREETINGS FROM
ALABAMA
FROM
Baltimore
MD.
Greetings
from
BOSTON
hello
FROM
SOUTH DAKOTA
Greetings from
Niagara
Falls
MEMPHIS
TENN.
Greetings
from
PHILADELPHIA
Pa.
Greetings
from
VIRGINIA
WASHINGTON

The Great American Road Trip

Eric Peterson

Publications International, Ltd.

A Denver-based freelance writer, **Eric Peterson** contributes to numerous periodicals and travel guides. His recent credits include the fifth edition of *Frommer's Montana & Wyoming* and stories for *Arthur Frommer's Budget Travel, EnCompass, and Westword.* When not on the road in search of oddities and adventure, he writes about business and technology and hikes the Rockies as often as he can.

Maps courtesy of Microsoft® Streets & Trips 2006 with GPS Locator **www.microsoft.com/streets.**

Special thanks to Wesley Treat (www.wesleytreat.com) for the use of photos on pages 139, 146, 149, 152, 153, 158–159.

Louis Weber, CEO
Publications International, Ltd.
7373 North Cicero Avenue
Lincolnwood, Illinois 60712

Manufactured in China.

8 7 6 5 4 3 2 1

ISBN-13: 978-1-4127-1183-8
ISBN-10: 1-4127-1183-5

Library of Congress Control Number: 2005924036

"I wanted to drive the American roads at the century's end, to look at the country again, from border to border and beach to beach . . ."

LARRY MCMURTRY, *ROADS: DRIVING AMERICA'S GREAT HIGHWAYS*

CONTENTS

Greetings From NORTH DAKOTA

THE EVOLUTION OF THE AMERICAN ROAD

THE FIRST TRANSCONTINENTAL roadway in the United States—the Abraham Lincoln Memorial Highway—was completed in 1915, connecting San Francisco with New York City. By 1925, named highways were everywhere, and the federal government approved a numbered system. That same year, the world's first motel opened for business in San Luis Obispo, California, charging $1.25 a night for room rental. For the first time, Americans enjoyed a truly independent mode of travel. A new era in tourism unofficially began: the era of the road trip.

By the 1940s, blacktop was snaking all over the United States. After World War II, highway construction picked up serious steam: People were buying cars, packing the kids in the backseat, and hitting the road with gleeful abandon. Motels, eateries, and gas stations opened along the highways. Savvy entrepreneurs searched for the best way to take advantage of increased auto traffic. Zipping along the highway, tourists needed—no, demanded—a reason to stop. The roadside pioneers needed to give the tourists something to gawk at. Before long, the shoulder of the road became populated with off-kilter creations of all kinds designed to get travelers to stop and spend some time, along with some of their vacation money. The more over-the-top and exaggerated a totem at highway's edge, the stronger its magnetism.

This book is dedicated to the far-flung folks whose passion—some may call it mania—slakes the nation's collective thirst for roadside

Firsts of the American Road

- **Speed limit:** No Galloping in New Amsterdam (now New York City), 1652
- **Federally funded highway:** The National Road (now U.S. 40), early 1800s
- **Transcontinental automobile trip:** Dr. Horatio Nelson Jackson, 1903
- **Transcontinental roadway:** Lincoln Highway, 1915
- **First drive-through restaurant:** Pig Stand, Dallas, Texas, 1921
- **Motel:** Milestone Motel, San Luis Obispo, California, 1925
- **Freeway:** Pasadena Freeway, California, 1940

kitsch with wild and wacky destinations lurking around every corner between the Pacific and Atlantic. You'll find Cadillac Ranch and the Ozymandias Leg Ruins in Texas, Wall Drug and the Corn Palace in South Dakota, New Jersey's Lucy the Elephant, and so many more. The goal is to show just why the American kitsch quest is so alluring.

Corn Palace
Mitchell, South Dakota

While the interstate system that developed in the latter part of the 20th century came as a fatal blow to many tourist landmarks, the heart of roadside Americana is still beating strong. The continent's seemingly endless highways remain loaded with grade-A roadside meccas—but people tend to whiz by on the superhighway instead of taking their time on the old two-laner. It takes something special to pull drivers off the unfettered interstate and into the rest of the world. But for those who do take the road less driven, this act is often its own reward.

The Rusty Bolt and Thunderbird Indian in Seligman, Arizona, is a favorite stop for travelers.

ROUTE 66—THE MOTHER ROAD

ROUTE 66 IS NOT remembered simply as a conduit between Chicago and Los Angeles, but as a passage to the heart of American cool—the last leg of the Manifest Destiny with a side helping of rock 'n' roll. With the convertible top down and the sun-soaked beaches of paradise somewhere over the horizon, day-to-day life was temporarily forgotten in the rearview mirror. Because the road snaked right through the heart of numerous cities and towns, the opportunities for fun (and trouble) were plentiful.

The sign says it all: Route 66 is part of America's history.

Now represented by a patchwork of interstates, two-laners, and decrepit stretches of asphalt, old Route 66 doesn't really exist, at least in the eyes of Congress or mapmakers. But it still exists for the nostalgic tourists—an unusual mix of bikers, travelers, and RVers—who stick as close as possible to the roads that were once Route 66 and see the old sights that have withstood the test of time.

CALIFORNIA

CALIFORNIA IS THE END of the road, where the blacktop slams to a halt at the beach and the Pacific Ocean. The state is in many ways the ultimate road-trip destination—temperate, idyllic, and jam-packed with world-class tourist draws.

En route from San Diego to the Redwood Coast, you can zip through Disneyland, Hollywood, and Haight-Ashbury and cruise the coastline all the way in between. This is where they make movies and microchips, where they grow everything from oranges to artichokes.

California's beaches are the stuff of legend; inland, its natural terrain varies from sizzling deserts to alpine peaks, from primeval forests to deep canyons. Culturally, it's similarly diverse, a true melting pot of everything from celebrity glamour to hippie chic.

Monterey Penninsula

Hollywood Sign

Hollywood

Before it became an icon of impending celebrity to newcomers with stars in their eyes, the Hollywood sign was a real estate promotion that actually read "Hollywood-land." The last four letters didn't survive, but the first nine did—albeit barely: By 1973, the sign was falling apart—one 'O' had toppled down the hill, and an arsonist had set fire to an 'L'—prompting a $250,000 reconstruction.

Happy Days

"Aaaayyyy!"

Though *Happy Days* was set in Milwaukee, the house used for the exterior shots of the Cunningham home is located at 565 N. Cahuenga Blvd. in West Hollywood.

Great Road-Trip Movies

- National Lampoon's *Vacation* (1983)
- *Easy Rider* (1969)
- *Dumb & Dumber* (1994)
- *Bonnie and Clyde* (1967)
- *Planes, Trains & Automobiles* (1987)
- *Thelma & Louise* (1991)
- *The Cannonball Run* (1981)
- *North By Northwest* (1959)
- *It's a Mad Mad Mad Mad World* (1963)
- *The Wizard of Oz* (1939)

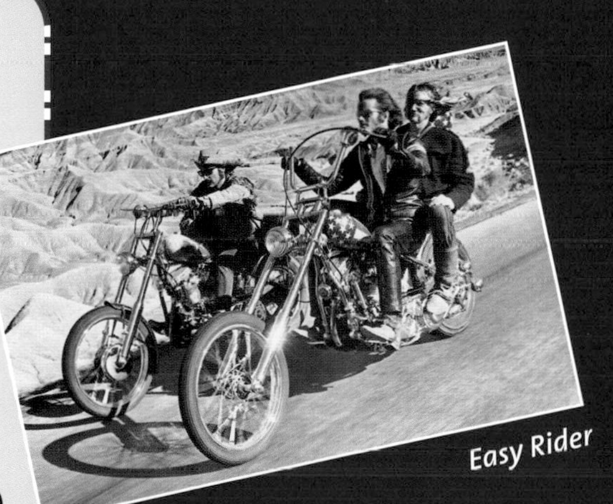
Easy Rider

Cornerstone Festival of Gardens

Sonoma

The founder of the first gallery-style garden exhibit in the United States, Chris Hougie, was inspired by the International Garden Festival at Chaumont-sur-Loire in France. The nine-acre Cornerstone brings to life the concept of landscape as art form and offers an ever-changing array of gardens and art that allows visitors to experience the work of the world's leading landscape architects. Sometimes surreal, sometimes cutting-edge, these gardens are always a pleasure to see.

Monterey Bay Aquarium

Monterey

The Monterey Bay Aquarium attracts more than a million visitors a year, and it's easy to see why. Located in the converted former Hovden Cannery (which canned squid and sardines until the early 1970s) on Monterey's legendary Cannery Row, the facility is the home of more than 550 species of plants and animals. Among the exhibits are live penguin shows and a living kelp forest.

Redwood National and State Parks

THE PRIMEVAL FORESTS of Redwood are home to some of the world's tallest trees, topping out at 367 feet. Everything is of an outsize scale here, from the banana slugs on the trail to the ferns growing next to it. The parks also include nearly 40 miles of unblemished coastline, frequented by sea lions, colonies of birds, and migrating gray whales.

Much of the development on U.S. 101 in the Redwood area feels like a holdover from a road trip of the past. Paul Bunyan stands sentry in front of the kitschy Trees of Mystery, while one-log structures, vintage roadside motels, and legends of Bigfoot abound.

Madonna Inn

San Luis Obispo

Proprietors Alex and Phyllis Madonna created an unforgettable lodging experience in this legendarily garish hotel that continues to grow and change. Each of the more than 100 rooms inside sports a different theme, ranging from the rock-clad Caveman Room to the deliriously pink Love Nest.

Bubblegum Alley

San Luis Obispo

Colorful, unusual, and a bit repulsive, the tradition of leaving one's chewing gum behind in Bubblegum Alley dates back to the 1960s. The alley is interactive and user-friendly: Several nearby downtown merchants conveniently have gum ball machines in front of their stores.

The California Coast

The primary north-south route on California's coast for the first half of the 20th century, U.S. 101 has since been bested by I-5 in terms of modernity, but not for providing a great road-trip adventure. The last stretch from Los Angeles to San Diego no longer exists as a true road, but travelers can still find surviving chunks of Old Highway 101 (and Highway 1) for a nostalgic look at the Southern California coast.

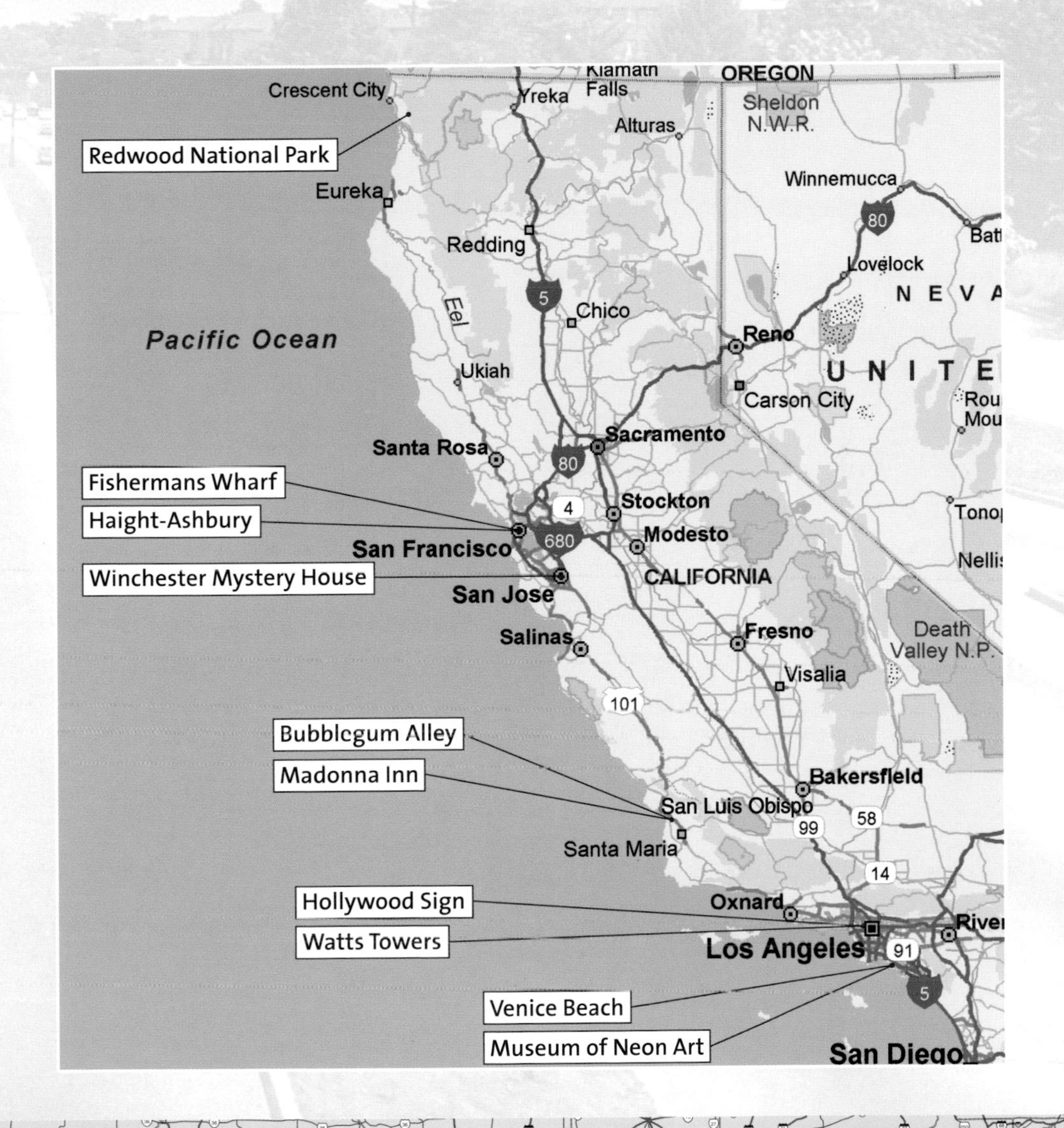
Redwood National Park
Fishermans Wharf
Haight-Ashbury
Winchester Mystery House
Bubblegum Alley
Madonna Inn
Hollywood Sign
Watts Towers
Venice Beach
Museum of Neon Art
Pacific Ocean
Crescent City
Yreka
Klamath Falls
Alturas
OREGON
Sheldon N.W.R.
Eureka
Redding
Winnemucca
Lovelock
Chico
Eel
Ukiah
Reno
Carson City
Sacramento
Santa Rosa
Stockton
Modesto
San Francisco
San Jose
CALIFORNIA
Salinas
Fresno
Death Valley N.P.
Visalia
Bakersfield
San Luis Obispo
Santa Maria
Oxnard
Los Angeles
San Diego

Fishermans Wharf

San Francisco

San Francisco's most popular tourist destination has been the heart of its fishing and crabbing industry for more than a century. Often accessed by the world-famous San Francisco cable cars, Fishermans Wharf is home to a plethora of tourist attractions, including a wax museum, an aquarium, a frolicking population of sea lions, and SBC Park, the home of baseball's San Francisco Giants.

"If you're alive, you can't be bored in San Francisco. If you're not alive, San Francisco will bring you to life."

WILLIAM SAROYAN

Thermometer

Baker

Rising from the searing sands of the Mojave Desert, this 134-foot thermometer is a towering tribute to the infamous day in 1913 when the temperature in Death Valley hit 134 degrees Fahrenheit. Replaced after the original was felled by high winds, the thermometer is the work of (and stands on the grounds of) the Bun Boy restaurant.

Artichoke

Castroville

Down the coast a bit from San Francisco, Castroville is the "Artichoke Center of the World," thanks to its famous Green Globe 'chokes and a $50 million local industry. The city pays homage to this distinction with this 20-foot-tall steel vegetable and an annual Artichoke Festival, which named Norma Jean Baker (aka Marilyn Monroe) its inaugural Artichoke Queen in 1947.

"Yosemite Valley, to me, is always a sunrise, a glitter of green and golden wonder in a vast edifice of stone and space."

ANSEL ADAMS

Yosemite National Park

- From winter through midsummer, Yosemite Falls is the longest waterfall in the country, gushing down 2,425 feet. By August, however, the falls completely dry up.

- Looming more than 3,000 feet over the floor of Yosemite Valley, El Capitan is the largest granite monolith in the world and a favorite spot for experienced rock climbers.

- Historic Yosemite Cemetery serves as a burial ground for Native Americans, early pioneers, and the occasional hapless park visitor. Headstones and monuments large and small tell the tales, including one that reads "In Memory of Effie Maud Crippen Died Aug 31st, 1881, Age 14 Yrs 7 Mos 22 Days, She faltered by the wayside and the angels took her home."

Haight-Ashbury

San Francisco

Centered on the famous intersection of Haight and Ashbury streets, the birthplace of hippie culture remains one of the grooviest neighborhoods on the planet, lined with beautiful Victorians (the Grateful Dead once called the one at 710 Ashbury home), funky shops, and bars and restaurants of every imaginable variety.

Integratron
Giant Rock

Built on a "magnetic vortex," a sonic chamber within the Integratron provides the venue for "sound baths" that supposedly rejuvenate the recipient. The visionary behind the Integratron, George Van Tassel, died before the domed structure near Joshua Tree National Park was completed. Its ability to lengthen life has never been tested, but it is open for tours (and sound baths) and rented out for special events.

JUMPING FROG JUBILEE

Angels Camp

MARK TWAIN WROTE "The Celebrated Jumping Frog of Calaveras County" in 1865, but it wasn't until 1928 that the first annual Jumping Frog Jubilee took place in Angels Camp, then a gold-rush town in decline. That year's winning jump was 3 feet, 6 inches, by the frog known as Pride of San Joaquin. The May event now attracts some 2,000 amphibious entrants a year.

"Optimist: Person who travels on nothing from nowhere to happiness." MARK TWAIN

WINCHESTER MYSTERY HOUSE

San Jose

IN 1884, a soothsayer told rifle heiress Sarah Winchester that she would die when she stopped building her house. Not daring to disbelieve the prediction, Winchester kept contractors busy working on her San Jose mansion for her remaining 38 years. The result is a maze of rooms, with stairways that lead to ceilings and doors that open to walls or to steep drops. One upper-story door opens directly to the outside!

When the hammering stopped after Sarah Winchester's death in 1922, there were:

160 rooms (including 40 bedrooms and 5 or 6 kitchens)

10,000 windows

950 doors

47 fireplaces

40 staircases

3 elevators

Watts Towers

Los Angeles

A definitive L.A. landmark, the collection of nine towers represents 35 years of work by Simon Rodia, a construction worker who moonlighted as a visionary artist and architect. After buying a triangular lot near the railroad tracks in 1921, Rodia dedicated his evenings and weekends to his solo project (without ever using power equipment) until he moved away in 1955. The city then ordered them demolished, but loving locals stepped in to save the mosaic-clad spires.

Museum of Neon Art

Los Angeles

Once nicknamed "liquid fire," neon has evolved into the ink of the American road. It's fitting that Los Angeles is home to the only museum dedicated to neon art—a Packard dealership here became home to the first neon signs in the United States in 1923. Founded in 1981, the Museum of Neon Art is located in downtown L.A.'s loft district. It plays host to several temporary exhibits each year and also offers classes in neon art and sign-seeing "cruises" of the neon-laden city.

Sequoia–Kings Canyon National Parks

Rugged and imposing, Sequoia Canyon National Park is home to the world's largest tree (by volume). The General Sherman Tree measures 275 feet high—and it's still growing! The General Sherman Tree is believed to be somewhere in the neighborhood of 2,000 years old, merely middle-aged by tree standards. The park is also home to the highest peak in the lower 48 states, 14,491-foot Mount Whitney. A glacial masterwork, Kings Canyon offers one of the most scenic drives anywhere, with sheer granite cliffs, sharp twists and turns, and dramatic waterfalls.

Cabazon Dinosaurs

Cabazon

While most dinosaur species haven't walked the earth in more than 60 million years, dinosaurs are far from extinct on the roadside. The most famous roadside dinosaurs are likely Claude Bell's brontosaurus and T-Rex (featured in Pee-wee's Big Adventure) along I-10 in Cabazon. Dinny, the giant brontosaurus, houses a small museum and gift shop in its belly. Since Bell died in 1989, their future has been shrouded in uncertainty.

HEARST CASTLE

San Simeon

OVER THE COURSE of nearly three decades, newspaper baron William Randolph Hearst built one of the most spectacular homes in the world on the 250,000-acre ranch he inherited in 1919. A prototype of Mediterranean Revival architecture, Hearst Castle is now operated by the California State Park System and is open for tours. Casa Grande, the 60,645-square-foot main house, features 115 rooms. Tours also include a trio of smaller abodes on the property: Casa del Mar, Casa del Monte, and Casa del Sol. The estate's 1,665-square-foot indoor Roman pool is modeled on an ancient Roman bath house and features marble replicas of eight Greek and Roman statues, while the magnificent outdoor Neptune Pool (above) is flanked by four 17th-century Italian bas-reliefs and holds 345,000 gallons of water.

"Miss Morgan, we are tired of camping out in the open at the ranch in San Simeon and I would like to build a little something . . . ."

WILLIAM RANDOLPH HEARST, TO ARCHITECT JULIA MORGAN

Venice Beach

NAMED AND MODELED AFTER Venice, Italy, when founded in the early 20th century, the Los Angeles neighborhood of Venice and the beach of the same name were once home to a Pacific cousin of New York's Coney Island. The amusement park is long gone, but Venice Beach in many ways remains the face of L.A. to the rest of the planet and the endpoint of many road trips.

Today, Venice Beach is one of the funkiest stretches of coastline in the country and a paradise for shoppers, surfers, people-watchers, and beach bums. Outdoor enthusiasts flock to Gold's Gym, a famous outdoor weight-lifting mecca, and a 22-mile bike and skating path along the beach.

Binocular Building

Just a few blocks from the boardwalk are a pair of landmark oddball buildings: an office building designed by Frank Gehry with a giant binoculars sculpture at the entrance (above), and the Venice Renaissance Building, which features a tutu-clad clown above the front door.

MARKET

THE PACIFIC NORTHWEST

CASCADIA, AS THIS AREA is called, is a fusion of nature and high technology. It has the continent's only temperate rain forest and supports fertile farmland, yet two-thirds of Oregon is high, parched desert. You'll find the caffeinated consciousness of its city dwellers, and the eco-awareness of those who celebrate the vast natural bounty of the area. The culture is definitely progressive...and is absolutely laid back.

Which all contributes to unforgettable roadside attractions—some of the most unusual in the country—and a fabulous opportunity to "Go West, Young Man (Woman, Child)."

Crater Lake National Park
Oregon

Space Needle

Seattle, Washington

Built as the centerpiece for the 1962 World's Fair, Seattle's Space Needle is still the most recognizable building in town. Initially a sketch on a place mat, the structure's now-retro design looks very much like a UFO perched atop three giant legs.

Experience Music Project

Seattle, Washington

In the shadow of the Space Needle lies the Experience Music Project (EMP), a museum devoted to the creation and enjoyment of all forms of music. The Frank Gehry–designed building is a curious mix of textures and colors meant to represent the fluid nature of music itself. Founder Paul Allen (who cofounded Microsoft with Bill Gates in 1975) drew inspiration for the EMP from his personal passion for music—he owns the largest collection of Jimi Hendrix memorabilia in the world.

Voodoo Doughnut

Portland, Oregon

More than a mere doughnut shop, Voodoo Doughnut is a night owl's dream—open from 10 P.M. to 10 A.M.—and a licensed wedding chapel. Their giant doughnuts come in a wide selection, from the namesake "Voodoo Doughnut" to the "Memphis Mafia" (with a peanut butter-banana-chocolate glaze). Doughnuts and coffee for ten are part of the wedding ceremony package.

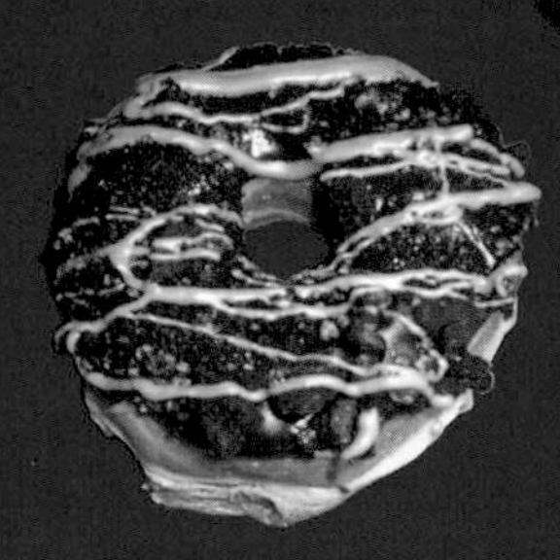

The Bomber

Milwaukie, Oregon

A World War II–era B-17G bomber graces this long-standing drive-in restaurant. The Bomber restaurant has been serving up thick milk shakes and Bomber Burgers since 1948, a year after Art Lacey bought the "flying fortress" and flew it to Oregon to use as an advertising gimmick for his gas station. Though the gas station closed in 1991, the restaurant is still run by Art Lacey's family.

Evel Knievel's Snake River Jump Site

Twin Falls, Idaho

AUTHORITIES FORBADE motorcycle daredevil Evel Knievel from jumping the Grand Canyon, so he looked north to Twin Falls, Idaho, and decided to give Snake River Canyon a try. Knievel's vehicle—the X-1 Skycycle, a two-wheeled hybrid of a motorcycle and a rocket ship—didn't quite make the 1,580 necessary feet on September 8, 1974, but with the help of a parachute Knievel landed safely on the canyon floor.

"I can say the Lord's prayer in 10 seconds."

Evel Knievel

Out 'n' About Treesort

Takilma, Oregon

Though it's a bit off the beaten path, this "treesort" promises an unforgettable experience—each unit is a different tree house. Each tree house has a different theme: You can choose to stay in the saloon-inspired "Treeloon," the "TreePee," the "Cavaltree Fort," or you can really go out on a limb and stay in the highest tree house, the 37-foot-high "Treezebo." If a whole night in a tree house is more than you want, take one of the daily tours of unoccupied units and the "Mountain View Treeway," a high-rise walkway that includes a 90-foot suspension bridge.

Petersen Rock Garden

Redmond, Oregon

Folk artist Rasmus Petersen created this four-acre rock garden as an homage to life in America. He started collecting rocks he found on his property, such as agate, obsidian, and malachite, in 1906 and began to build monuments, bridges, and buildings in 1935. The garden features replicas of the Statue of Liberty and Independence Hall, and the adjoining museum offers a fluorescent rock display.

The Miner's Hat

Kellogg, Idaho

The onetime mining hotbed of the Silver Valley is a natural home for this structure, shaped like a miner's hat with a carbide lamp, at the foot of mountains once scoured for silver and gold. Originally a drive-in restaurant, the building has housed the offices of Miner's Hat Realty since the 1960s.

Hat 'n' Boots gas station

Seattle, Washington

A landmark in Seattle's Georgetown neighborhood, the massive hat and boots once housed a service station office and restrooms, respectively. After a lengthy stay on Route 99 (Route 66's sister road), the establishment shut down in 1988 and was the victim of roadside neglect. But a grassroots movement to save it emerged in the 1990s, and the hat and boots were restored and relocated to nearby Oxbow Park in 2003.

Seattle to Mount Rainier

WHEN THE CLOUDS AROUND Seattle part, locals like to say, "The mountain is out today," meaning one can see the majestic 14,410-foot Mount Rainier, an active volcano encased in ice and snow. Road-trippers can do better by hopping in the car and driving a couple of hours to get up close and personal with "the mountain."

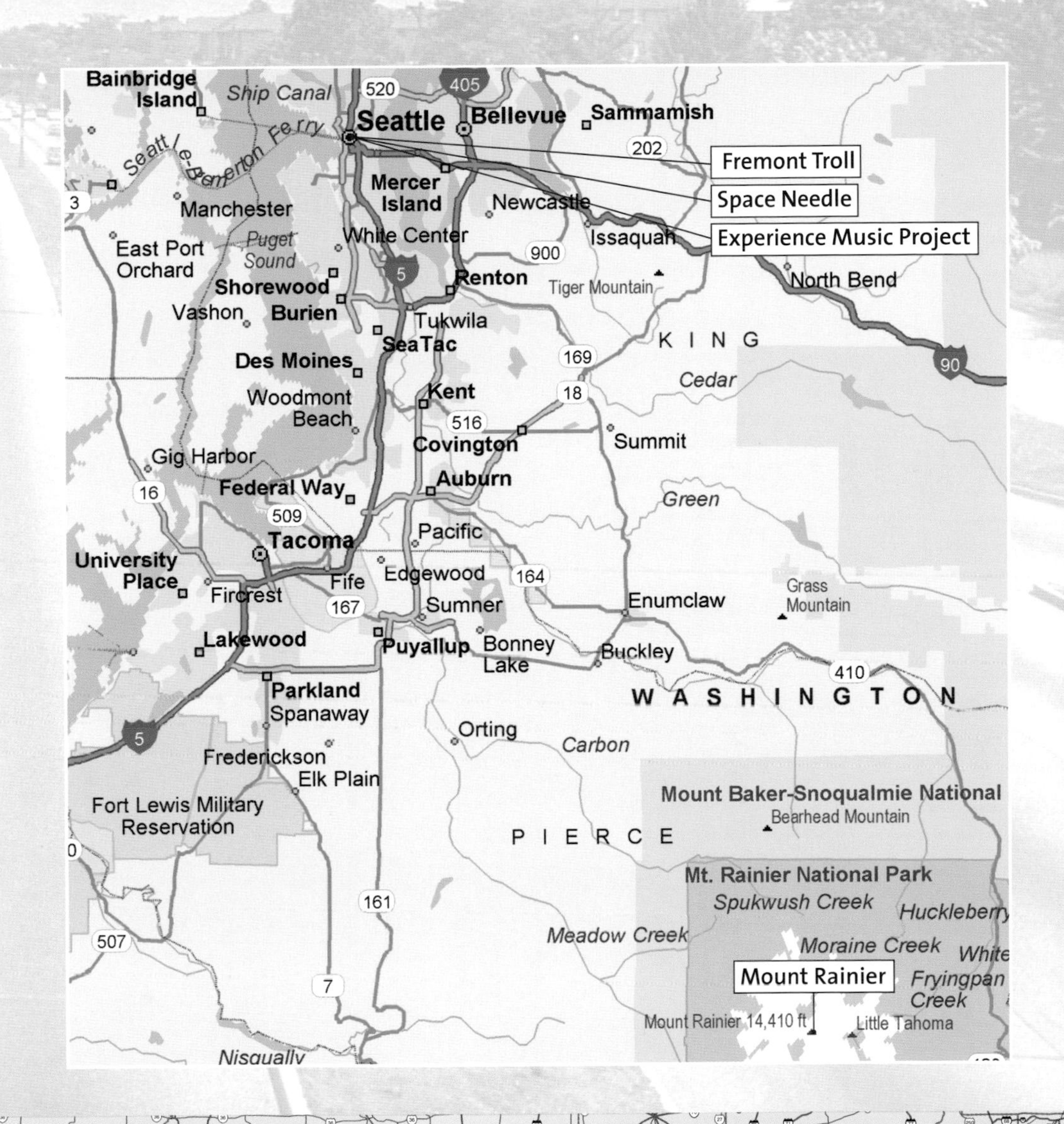

Bainbridge Island
Ship Canal
520
405
Seattle
Bellevue
Sammamish
Seattle-Bremerton Ferry
202
Fremont Troll
Space Needle
Experience Music Project
3
Manchester
Mercer Island
Newcastle
East Port Orchard
Puget Sound
White Center
Issaquah
900
Shorewood
5
Renton
Tiger Mountain
North Bend
Vashon
Burien
Tukwila
SeaTac
K I N G
Des Moines
169
90
Cedar
Woodmont Beach
Kent
18
516
Covington
Summit
Gig Harbor
Auburn
16
Federal Way
Green
509
Tacoma
Pacific
University Place
Edgewood
164
Fircrest
Fife
167
Sumner
Enumclaw
Grass Mountain
Lakewood
Puyallup
Bonney Lake
Buckley
410
Parkland
Spanaway
W A S H I N G T O N
Orting
Carbon
Fredrickson
Elk Plain
Fort Lewis Military Reservation
Mount Baker-Snoqualmie National
Bearhead Mountain
P I E R C E
Mt. Rainier National Park
Spukwush Creek
Huckleberry
161
507
Meadow Creek
Moraine Creek
White
Mount Rainier
Fryingpan Creek
7
Mount Rainier 14,410 ft
Little Tahoma
Nisqually

Archie McPhee

Seattle, Washington

A local favorite since it opened in 1983, Archie McPhee is a superstore for the strange, overflowing with the oddest oddities on the market. The bizarre bazaar sells everything from latex lizards to blue beehive wigs to bacon-scented air fresheners—if it's weird, this place has it.

"The whole object of travel is not to set foot on foreign land; it is at last to set foot on one's own country as a foreign land."

GILBERT KEITH CHESTERTON

FUNNY FARM

Bend, Oregon

THIS RAMSHACKLE RECYCLED roadside park includes a totem pole made out of tires, a garden sprouting bowling balls (seeds available in the gift shop), and an unusual kaleidoscope that shows *The Wizard of Oz* over and over—and that's just scratching the surface. There's also a goat-racing field, a pink flamingo nesting area, and a "Love Pond" with a giant arrow piercing its depths.

Pink flamingo nest

Bowling ball garden

Fremont Troll

Seattle, Washington

Like a postmodern Brothers Grimm tale, a gigantic concrete troll lurks under the Aurora Avenue Bridge in Seattle's Fremont neighborhood, mangling a Volkswagen Beetle in its massive meat hook. That location had been increasingly littered with junk before the troll was built, and the Fremont Arts Council revitalized the area, making it the epicenter of the neighborhood's burgeoning troll culture.

Caveman

Grants Pass, Oregon

In 1874, a hunter uncovered a cave system near Grants Pass. The men in the community eventually used it as the launching pad for an Elks-like club named the Cavemen. After a secret subterranean ceremony in 1922, the group dressed in skins and marched in local parades. The club isn't as visible today, but members left a lasting mark on the town in the form of an 18-foot fiberglass Neanderthal who welcomes visitors.

Red Wagon

Spokane, Washington

Located above the Spokane River in Riverfront Park, this enormous (12 feet high and 27 feet long) red Radio Flyer wagon can hold a small army of children—the maximum capacity is 300. Named *The Childhood Express,* the 26-ton plaything is an interactive monument to childhood: Visitors can climb up a ladder on the back and slide down the handle.

Hobo Inn

Elbe, Washington

Near the foot of majestic Mount Rainier, the Hobo Inn is the place to bed down for the night for an experience that melds creature comforts with the hobo lifestyle. The proprietors have converted about a half-dozen vintage cabooses into motel rooms (bindle on a stick not included).

"I have found out that there ain't no surer way to find out whether you like people or hate them than to travel with them."

Mark Twain

Teapot Dome gas station

Zillah, Washington

Built as a comic rebuttal to the Teapot Dome oil deals—a salacious political scandal of the 1920s—this is said to be the country's oldest operating gas station. Shaped like a 15-foot-tall teapot, the building is one of the most recognizable structures along I-82 in southern Washington.

ALASKA AND HAWAII

THE MERE MENTION OF Alaska and Hawaii conjures romantic images of faraway destinations. Alaska—named for the Russian interpretation of the Aleutian word *alakshak,* or "great lands"—is the country's vast arctic frontier, a wild place that's nearly ten times the size of an average state. There aren't many roads to cover the large area, but on the plus side the traffic is usually light.

It's difficult to transport a car to Hawaii, but a rental offers road-trip rewards in the form of lush landscapes, active volcanoes, and tropical weather. There are eight islands in all, including Kauai, Oahu, Maui, and the "Big Island" of Hawaii. This is the realm of the pineapple, the surfboard, and the road trip to paradise.

St. Elias National Park
Alaska

IOLANI PALACE

Honolulu, Hawaii

BUILT IN 1882, Iolani Palace is the only royal palace in the United States and was the official residence of the Hawaiian Kingdom's last two monarchs. King Kalakaua, who had the palace built, was succeeded by his sister, Queen Lili'uokalani, who was overthrown in 1893 and imprisoned in a palace bedroom for five years. This ornate and opulent palace is now open for tours.

Santa Claus House

North Pole, Alaska

In the early 1950s, Con and Nellie Miller relocated to Alaska. Mr. Miller wore an old red Santa suit and soon became "Santa" in the eyes of local children. The name caught on, and the couple built this gift shop and trading post to celebrate the spirit of Christmas all year. A giant Santa marks the entrance to the shop, and reindeer can be found on the grounds. You can even order a personalized letter from Santa proclaiming the recipient to be on the "Good List."

Igloo City Resort

Cantwell, Alaska

The icelike exterior of this four-story igloo located between Fairbanks and Anchorage sheaths an unfinished interior: The developers ran out of money before the planned grand opening of the ill-fated resort. Regardless, the place is a hard-to-miss monument to what could have been, with a gas station and gift shop in lieu of rooms for rent.

The Road to Hana

It's only about 50 miles from the Maui airport to the isolated coastal village of Hana, but the drive usually takes more than two hours. In this case, the longer, the better: The Hana Highway is a road worth savoring, winding through a tropical rain forest laden with waterfall-fed swimming holes and jaw-dropping panoramas. Hana itself offers both red cinder and black sand beaches, rugged cliffs, botanic gardens, and a cultural center.

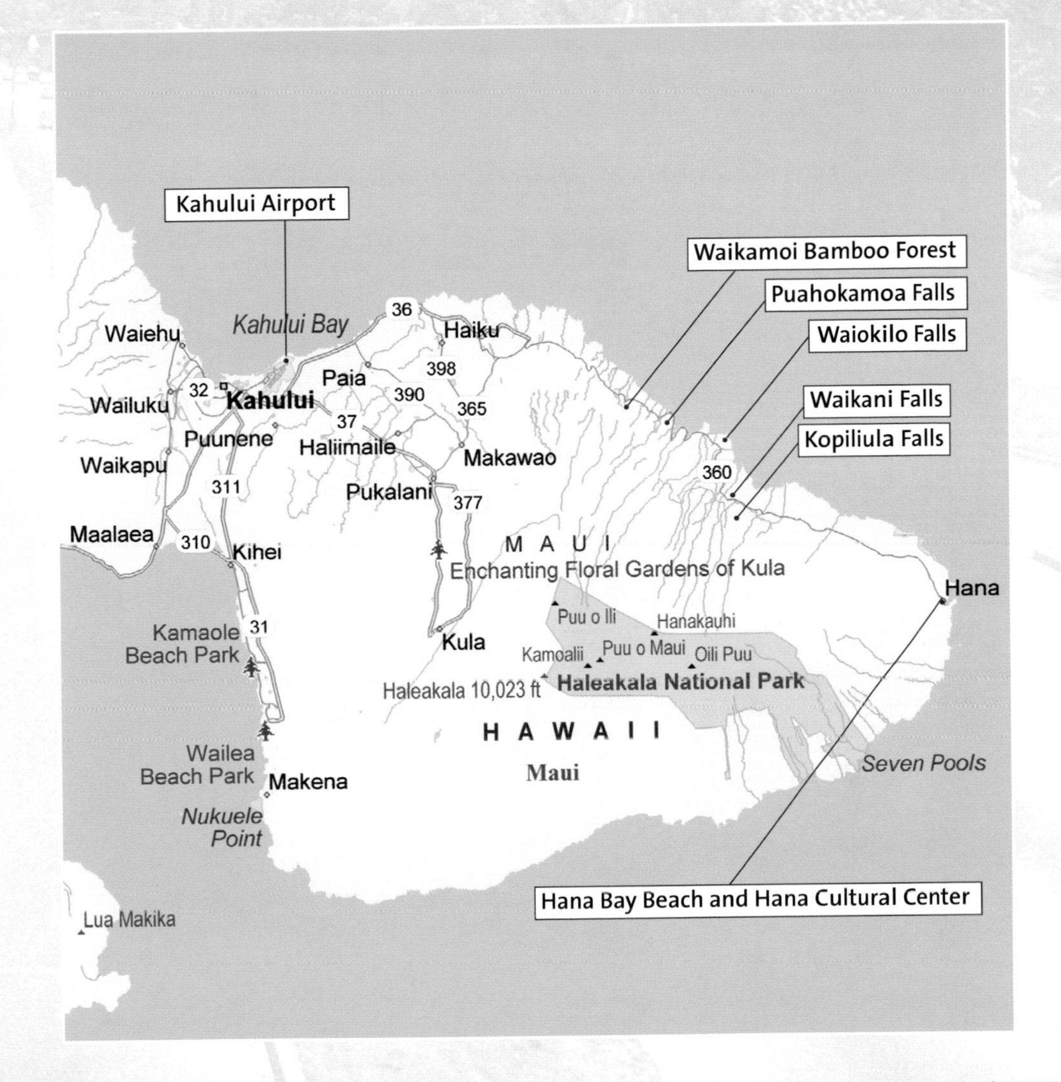

Kahului Airport
Waikamoi Bamboo Forest
Puahokamoa Falls
Waiokilo Falls
Waikani Falls
Kopiliula Falls
Kahului Bay
Waiehu
36
Haiku
398
Paia
32
Kahului
Wailuku
390
365
37
Puunene
Haliimaile
Makawao
Waikapu
360
311
Pukalani
377
Maalaea
310
Kihei
M A U I
Enchanting Floral Gardens of Kula
Hana
Puu o Ili
Hanakauhi
Kamaole Beach Park
31
Kula
Kamoalii
Puu o Maui
Oili Puu
Haleakala 10,023 ft
Haleakala National Park
H A W A I I
Wailea Beach Park
Makena
Maui
Seven Pools
Nukuele Point
Hana Bay Beach and Hana Cultural Center
Lua Makika

WORLD ICE ART CHAMPIONSHIPS

Fairbanks, Alaska

ORIGINATING IN THE 1930s as the Fairbanks Winter Carnival and Dog Derby, the World Ice Art Championships evolved into an annual tradition in the late 1980s. Teams from all over the world carve blocks of ice into ornate sculptures of all kinds. Over the years, sculptures have included stingrays, dragons, 100-foot towers, and truly inspired abstract works. The blocks used are harvested from a frozen pond; past events have used 1,500 tons of ice.

Ice sculptors

TOP TEN BEACHES IN AMERICA

(2004)

Dr. Beach (aka Dr. Stephen Leatherman), a professor of environmental sciences at Florida International University, publishes an annual list of the top beaches in the United States.

1. Hanauma Bay, Oahu, Hawaii
2. Fort De Soto Park, Florida
3. Ocracoke Island, North Carolina
4. Caladesi Island State Park, Florida
5. Main Beach, East Hampton, New York
6. Hanalei Bay, Kauai, Hawaii
7. Crescent Beach, Siesta Key, Florida
8. Coast Guard Beach, Cape Cod, Massachusetts
9. Cape Florida State Park, Florida
10. Coronado Beach, California

Hanalei Bay
Kauai, Hawaii

Hanauma Bay
Oahu, Hawaii

Hawaii Volcanoes National Park

This is the spot to get up close—but not *too* close—to active volcanoes on the "Big Island" of Hawaii. Lava streams in the park have been known to destroy roads, but they also act as creators—after all, it took 70 million years of volcanism to make Hawaii what it is today.

Denali National Park

Also known as Mt. McKinley, the 20,320-foot-tall Denali ("High One" in the native Athabascan tongue) is the tallest mountain in North America. The renowned wildlife population here includes grizzly bears, gray wolves, caribou, and moose. There are no reptiles and just one amphibian species, the wood frog, which actually freezes solid in winter and waits without breath or heartbeat until spring.

THE SOUTHWEST

IN THE LAND OF blackjack, spicy salsa, and untamed desert, the summer heat gives way to perfect falls and mild winters. The Southwest in December is downright cozy in comparison to more frosty climes—which makes the region perfect for a winter road trip.

The weather is just one lure. There's also the gambling and nightlife in Nevada and the Grand Canyon, Canyon de Chelly, and the saguaro forests of Arizona. New Mexico has its share of natural wonders, not to mention great arts destinations and legends of UFOs. And Oklahoma has some great roadside attractions of its own.

Grand Canyon
Arizona

TINKERTOWN

Sandia Park, New Mexico

A LIFETIME OF CARVING and collecting by the late Ross Ward is the bedrock for a sprawling and charmingly eclectic tourist attraction northeast of Albuquerque on Old Route 66. The museum is surrounded by barricades fashioned from bottles and includes a miniature town—Tinkertown—that Ward began carving in the early 1960s.

A quirky wooden band provides a glimpse of the wonderful oddities housed in Tinkertown.

A small section of the rambling walls that surround the museum.

"I did all this while you were watching TV."

ROSS WARD

Blue Whale

Catoosa, Oklahoma

Hugh Davis originally built this happy beast as an anniversary present for his wife in the early 1970s. The 80-foot smiling cement whale attracted so much attention on Route 66 that it became the showpiece for a reptile zoo and swimming hole operated by Davis until shortly before his death. The community has since rallied around the landmark, refurbishing it and applying thousands of gallons of blue paint in the process.

Totem Pole Park

Foyil, Oklahoma

It took Ed Galloway 11 years, adding one bucket of cement at a time, to create the centerpiece to his park. The 90-foot-tall tribute to American Indians has more than 200 different carvings on its facade, and its base is a stout 18 feet in diameter.

THE STRIP

Las Vegas, Nevada

THE NEON FRENZY of Sin City has been the inspiration for countless road trips. Here, a roll of the dice can make the difference between a mortgage payment and foreclosure. Who needs to travel the world when a simple drive down Las Vegas Boulevard leads to Paris, New York, and Monte Carlo?

The Bellagio

The Bellagio Hotel is fronted by a series of enormous fountains that shoot water as high as 240 feet in the air. At various times each day, the fountains are the star of their own choreographed water and light show.

Las Vegas to the Grand Canyon

Little White Chapel
Las Vegas, Nevada

A ROAD TRIP OF EXTREMES, this route starts in what might be the zenith of the artificial—Las Vegas. The drive passes by a little desert kitsch en route to the Grand Canyon, a masterwork crafted by nature for eons.

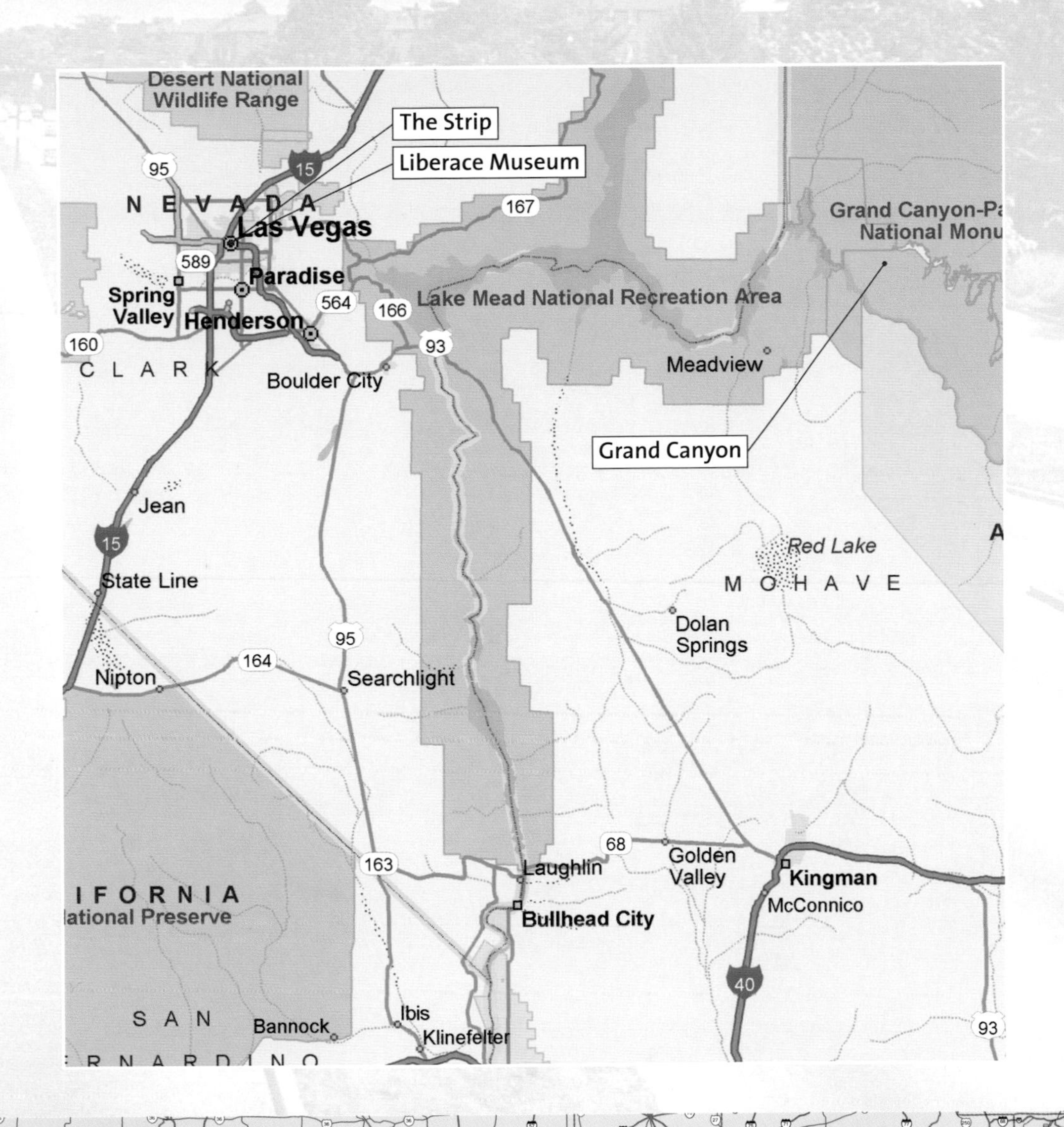
Desert National Wildlife Range
The Strip
Liberace Museum
NEVADA
Las Vegas
Paradise
Spring Valley
Henderson
CLARK
Boulder City
Lake Mead National Recreation Area
Meadview
Grand Canyon-Pa
National Monu
Grand Canyon
Jean
State Line
Red Lake
MOHAVE
Dolan Springs
Nipton
Searchlight
Laughlin
Golden Valley
Kingman
McConnico
Bullhead City
IFORNIA
lational Preserve
SAN
Bannock
Ibis
Klinefelter
95
15
167
589
564
166
93
160
164
163
68
40

O.K. Corral

Tombstone, Arizona

The O.K. Corral is the site of one of the most famous gunfights in the history of the Wild West. In 1881, Wyatt, Virgil, and Morgan Earp, along with Doc Holliday, engaged in a 30-second shootout with the McLaury and Clanton brothers. Restored to its 1880s image, the O.K. Corral features daily reenactments of the gunfight.

Great Wild West Destinations

- Gunfighters Wax Museum, Dodge City, Kansas
- Buffalo Bill Museum, Cody, Wyoming
- Billy the Kid's boyhood home, Silver City, New Mexico
- Boot Hill Graveyard, Tombstone, Arizona
- Broken Boot Gold Mine, Deadwood, South Dakota
- Charles M. Russell Museum, Great Falls, Montana
- Judge Roy Bean Visitor Center, Langtry, Texas
- Matchless Mine, Leadville, Colorado
- Crystal Palace Saloon, Tombstone, Arizona

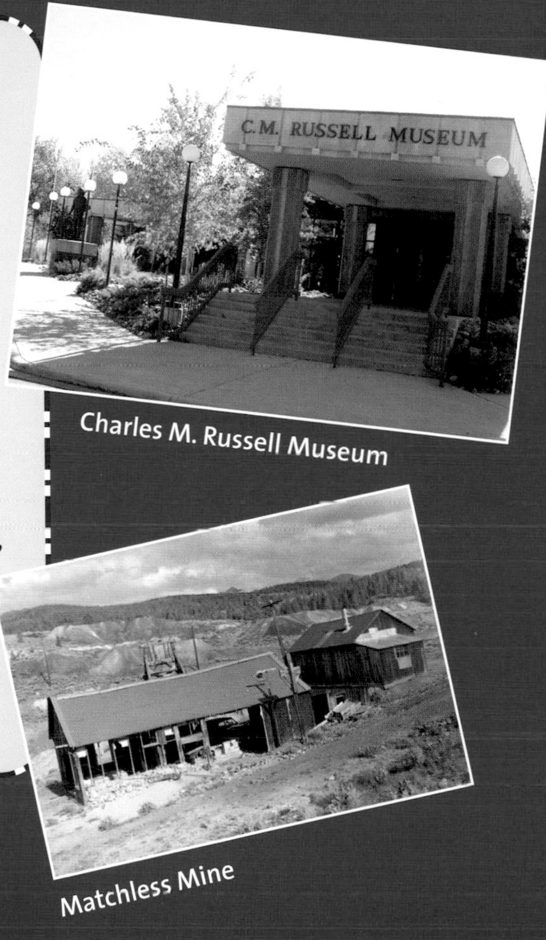

Charles M. Russell Museum

Matchless Mine

BURNING MAN

Near Gerlach, Nevada

AN ANNUAL TRADITION SINCE 1986, Burning Man started as a small group of people burning an eight-foot wooden figure on a San Francisco beach to celebrate the summer solstice. In the 21st century, the event has evolved into a week-long gathering in Nevada's Black Rock Desert, attended by more than 25,000 people and featuring a Burning Man that often tops 50 feet.

The main principles of Burning Man are self-reliance and expression. The temporary community, known as Black Rock City, encourages the creation and sharing of art in all forms, from large-scale installations to crafts to musical performances. Participants barter or give away art and supplies, but in keeping with the theme of self-reliance, the only products that are sold at Burning Man are coffee and ice.

The "Painted People" express themselves through dance.

International UFO Museum and Research Center

Roswell, New Mexico

The International UFO Museum is ground zero for the controversy surrounding the events of July 1947, when a UFO allegedly crashed in the countryside near Roswell. It's the centerpiece of the city's downtown and the natural starting point for an alien-related vacation of any kind.

Great American Paranormal Sites

- International UFO Museum, Roswell, New Mexico
- Bigfoot Museum, Willow Creek, California
- Champ the Sea Monster, Lake Champlain, New York
- UFO Watchtower, Hooper, Colorado
- Marfa Mystery Lights, Marfa, Texas
- Mystery Spot, Santa Cruz, California
- Little A'Le'Inn, Rachel, Nevada

Roswell, New Mexico

UFO Museum

Four Corners Marker

Colorado; New Mexico; Arizona; Utah

A painted concrete slab in the heart of the Navajo Nation marks the only point in the United States where four state boundaries intersect. The nominal admission charge is a small price to pay for the privelige of placing each extremity in a different state at the same time.

London Bridge

Lake Havasu City, Arizona

After local authorities determined the old London Bridge was sinking into the Thames River, the crumbling granite went up for auction as plans were drawn for a replacement. The winning bidder—Lake Havasu City founder Robert McCulloch—paid about $2.5 million for the old one, then shipped it to Long Beach, trucked it to Arizona, and rebuilt it over a manufactured lagoon as a tourist attraction.

"The one great sight every American should see."
Theodore Roosevelt

GRAND CANYON

THE TRUE MAGNIFICENCE of the Grand Canyon takes all visitors by surprise—nothing in the topography on either side gives a hint of what is soon to unfold. The chasm is so vast and so deep that on first sight it looks as though the earth has opened to allow a glimpse of the secrets that lie at its greatest depths.

Duck-on-a-Rock formation

Longhorn Grill

Amado, Arizona

It's difficult to imagine a restaurant more western than one shaped like a giant longhorn skull. That's the case at the Longhorn Grill, a desert outpost eatery located in the saguaro-studded sands between Tucson, Arizona, and Nogales, Mexico. Besides functioning as a restaurant, the building has been used as a location for several movies, including *Alice Doesn't Live Here Anymore*.

Shady Dell RV Park

Bisbee, Arizona

A commercial outpost and campground on Arizona 80 since the Roaring Twenties, Shady Dell is now one part traditional RV park and one part blast from the past. The latter: five unblemished vintage trailers dating from 1949 to 1954, their interiors bedecked with nostalgic decor. Also on-site is Dot's Diner, a 1950s eatery relocated to the Arizona desert from L.A.

LIBERACE MUSEUM

Las Vegas, Nevada

THE LATE "MR. SHOWMANSHIP," Liberace was a Las Vegas legend known for both tickling the ivories and his over-the-top style. The museum that bears his name reflects his love for all things extravagant with collections of his cars, costumes, and pianos. Highlights include a Rolls-Royce sheathed entirely in mirrored tiles and etched with images of horses, a gold ring in the shape of a piano decorated with 260 diamonds, and hundreds of costumes, ranging from a mink cape lined with rhinestones to a 200-pound aquatic-themed costume.

"I had to dare a little bit. Who am I kidding—I had to dare a lot. Don't wear one ring, wear five or six. People ask how I can play with all those rings, and I reply, 'Very well, thank you.'"

LIBERACE

Golden Driller

Tulsa, Oklahoma

Originally erected for the International Petroleum Exposition, the Golden Driller claims the title of world's largest free-standing statue—76 feet tall and 43,500 pounds. The big guy was refurbished and relocated to its current home at the Tulsa Exposition Center in 1966, where it has since survived tornadoes, art critics, and even the occasional shotgun blast.

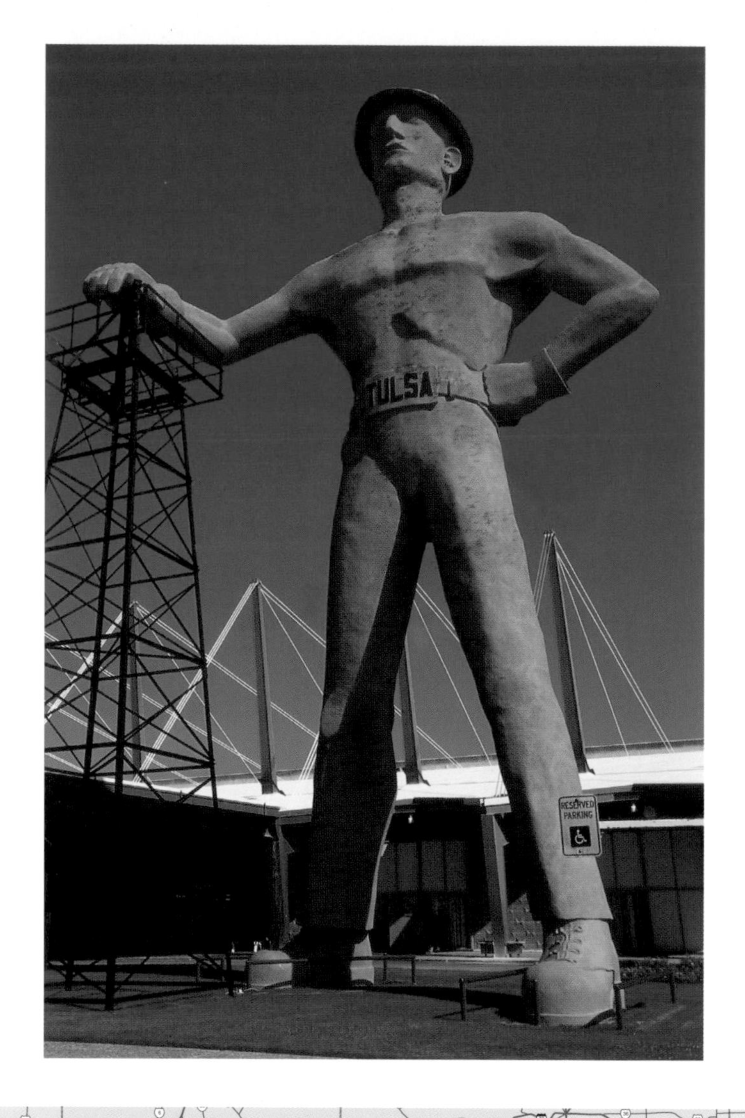

Claims Stake Prospector

Washoe Valley, Nevada

This 18-foot-tall prospector brandishes an oversize chunk of faux gold in order to attract chocoholics to the Chocolate Nugget Candy Factory, located between Reno and Carson City on U.S. 395. Before his stint hawking candy, he was the mascot of the Prospector, a casino/hotel in nearby Sparks.

THE ROCKIES

THE ROCKIES ARE JUST the place to get lost on a road trip, with mythic scenery and wide-open spaces. Most of the region, especially Wyoming and Montana, remains crowd-free. Even relatively large cities such as Denver and Salt Lake City seem isolated by all the space around them. Beyond city limits the road beckons, and roadside attractions are found in some out-of-the-way places.

Hitter's Tower
Arches National Park, Utah

SWETSVILLE ZOO

Timnath, Colorado

A FARMER BY TRADE, Bill Swets began crafting his unique sculptures as a cure for insomnia. Now his zoo—a stone's throw from I-25—is populated with real and imagined beasts of all kinds, made from old car parts, farm equipment, and other industrial scraps. The menagerie runs the gamut from a swan made out of a motorcycle gas tank to a scrap-metal version of Snoopy on his doghouse to a three-piece "heavy metal" alligator band.

Bird sculptures

Left: The driveway to the Swets castle is lined with sculptures.
Above: A metal golfer tees off near dinosaurs.

Casa Bonita

Denver, Colorado

Said to be the largest restaurant in the Western Hemisphere (at 52,000 square feet!), Denver's Casa Bonita is one of the last vestiges of a regional chain of Mexican theme restaurants. The exterior, clad in pink stucco with a gilded dome tower that houses a statue of the Aztec Emperor Quahuatomec, masks an even more outrageous interior: faux cliffs, faux caverns, and long lines for cafeteria-style Mexican dinners.

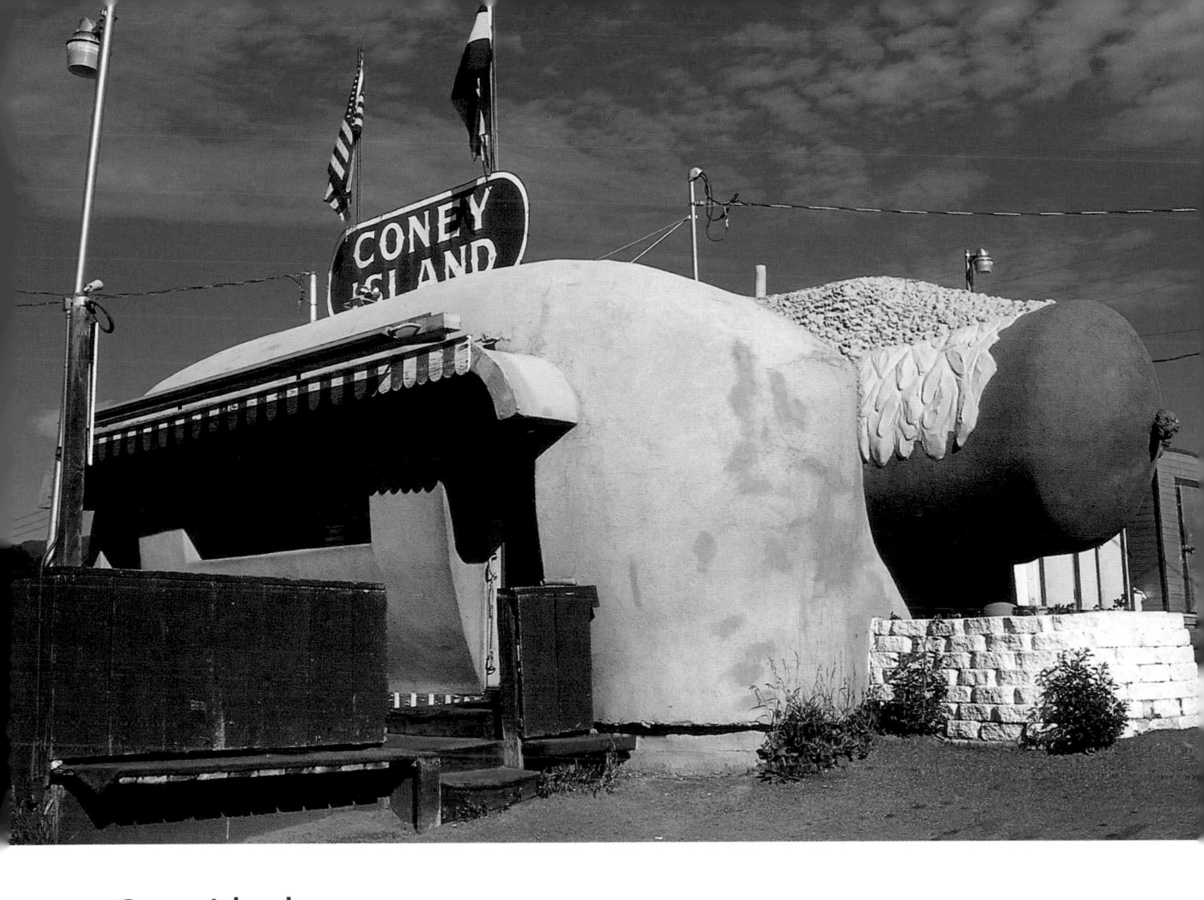

Coney Island

Aspen Park, Colorado

This hot dog–shape building is, not too surprisingly, a hot dog stand. While it actually began life on Colfax Avenue in Denver, it was relocated from its urban birthplace to the Rocky Mountain foothills in 1969 and has been a red-hot landmark en route to the great outdoors ever since.

Denver to Rocky Mountain National Park

AFTER LUNCH AT CASA BONITA, speed through Boulder en route to the rooftop of the continent, where Trail Ridge Road snakes across the Continental Divide and through the alpine tundra. No road trip to the Rockies is complete without navigating this winding strip of blacktop. On the way out, detour to the Swetsville Zoo and the Great Stupa of Dharmakaya for a worthwhile side trip.

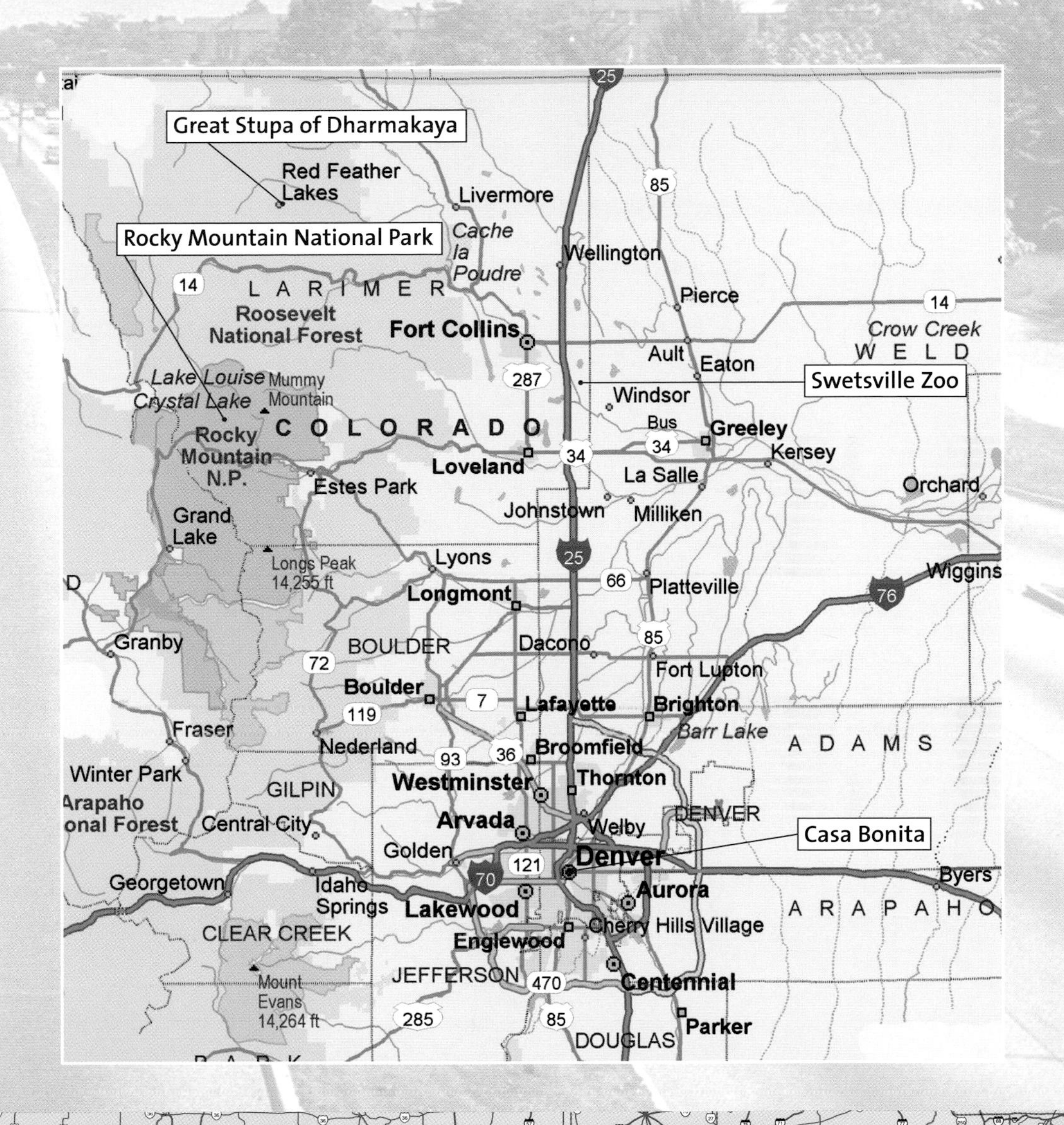

Great Stupa of Dharmakaya
Rocky Mountain National Park
Swetsville Zoo
Casa Bonita
Red Feather Lakes
Livermore
Cache la Poudre
Wellington
Pierce
LARIMER
Roosevelt National Forest
Fort Collins
Ault
Eaton
Crow Creek
WELD
Windsor
Lake Louise
Crystal Lake
Mummy Mountain
COLORADO
Rocky Mountain N.P.
Estes Park
Loveland
Bus
Greeley
Kersey
La Salle
Orchard
Johnstown
Milliken
Grand Lake
Longs Peak 14,255 ft
Lyons
Longmont
Platteville
Wiggins
Granby
BOULDER
Dacono
Fort Lupton
Boulder
Lafayette
Brighton
Barr Lake
Fraser
Nederland
Broomfield
ADAMS
Winter Park
GILPIN
Westminster
Thornton
Arapaho
onal Forest
Central City
Arvada
Welby
DENVER
Golden
Denver
Georgetown
Idaho Springs
Lakewood
Aurora
Byers
ARAPAHO
CLEAR CREEK
Cherry Hills Village
Englewood
JEFFERSON
Centennial
Mount Evans 14,264 ft
Parker
DOUGLAS
25
85
14
287
34
66
76
72
7
119
93
36
121
70
470
285

The Great Stupa of Dharmakaya

Red Feather Lakes, Colorado

TUCKED IN THE MOUNTAINS northwest of Fort Collins, Colorado, this is the largest stupa—a monument to a great Buddhist teacher—in North America. Dedicated to the late Chogyam Trungpa, the 108-foot spire is a work of ornate and symbolic art. It was built with a special formulation of concrete designed to last more than 1,000 years.

"You cannot travel the path until you
have become the path itself." BUDDHA

Penguin

Cut Bank, Montana

Commemorating its hometown's status as the coldest town in the United States, this concrete penguin is 27 feet tall and weighs a solid five tons. It beckons to passersby from its spot in front of the Glacier Gateway Inn, a furniture-shop-turned-motel. The penguin talks (when its speaker works), bleating out the slogan, "Welcome to Cut Bank, the coldest spot in the nation!"

Hercules Beetle

Colorado Springs, Colorado

This imposing Hercules beetle is the mascot of—and turnoff marker to—the John May Museum Center, best known for its permanent collection of about 100,000 insect specimens. Fittingly, Hercules beetles are also the world's largest real-life beetles, bugs so big (up to 6¾ inches long!) they've knocked down people unlucky enough to be in their flight path.

HOLE N" THE ROCK

Moab, Utah

IN THE 1940S AND '50s, Albert Christensen carved right into a red sandstone formation south of Moab, chipping away until his death in 1957 to create a 5,000-square-foot home and gift shop. Just a short trip from Arches and Canyonlands national parks, the place is today a funky trading post and roadside attraction where you can still see the 65-foot chimney Christensen drilled as well as the bathtub he carved out of solid rock.

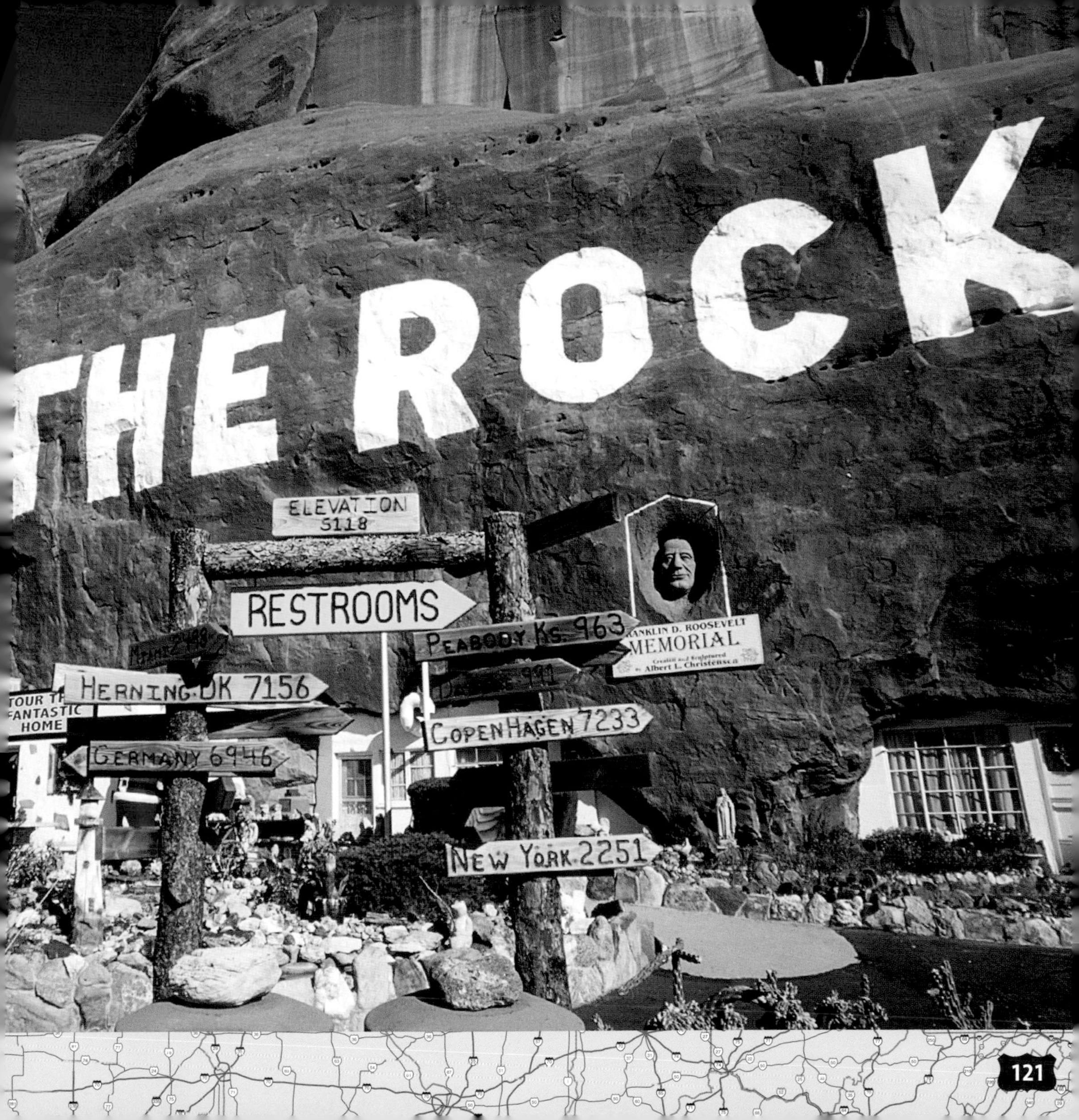
THE ROCK
ELEVATION
5118
RESTROOMS
PEABODY KS. 963
MEMORIAL
HERNING DK 7156
FANTASTIC
HOME
GERMANY 6946
COPENHAGEN 7233
NEW YORK 2251

BUFFALO BILL'S GRAVE

Golden, Colorado

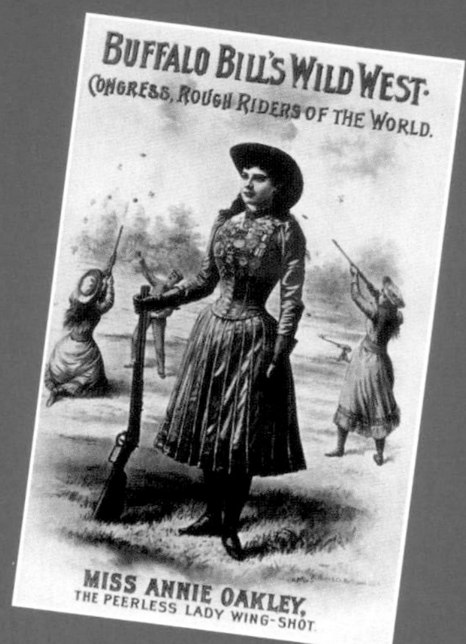

THE FINAL RESTING SPOT of Wild West performer William "Buffalo Bill" Cody is on Lookout Mountain—or maybe not. According to legend, a few of Cody's friends swapped his body with that of an anonymous cowboy and buried him just outside the town that he founded, Cody, Wyoming. Regardless, the official grave in Colorado was protected by National Guard troops for a spell before an impenetrable layer of concrete was poured over the site.

WILLIAM FREDERICK CODY
"BUFFALO BILL"
1846 — 1917
LOUISA MAUD CODY
1844 — 1921
COL. WM. F. CODY
LOUISA FREDERICI CODY

Jackalope

Douglas, Wyoming

Douglas, Wyoming, is the self-proclaimed "Jackalope Capital of the World" because, as the tall tale goes, pioneers first spotted the legendary critter there in the 1820s. The city pays homage to the beast with a statue in the center of town and an annual festival. Jackalope hunting licenses are even available through the local chamber of commerce, but only to those whose IQ is more than 50 but less than 72, and the season is limited to two hours a year.

Mike the Headless Chicken

Fruita, Colorado

In 1945, Lloyd Olsen chopped a chicken's head off but missed its brain stem. Rather than getting fried, the bird, dubbed "Mike the Headless Chicken," lived for another 18 months, with Olsen feeding it with an eyedropper. Sculptor Lyle Nichols paid tribute to Mike's fortitude with this 300-pound interpretation, and the city of Fruita also plays host to an annual festival that invites visitors to "party their heads off."

ARCHES NATIONAL PARK

Utah

A FANTASYLAND IN ROCK, Arches National Park is filled with giant balanced rocks that look as though they are about to teeter and fall. There are pedestals and spires that resemble a child's sand castles expanded to enormous scale. Chiseled by the powerful forces of wind and water, this surprising natural rock garden contains one of the foremost collections of abstract sculpture in the world.

North Window

Bishop Castle

Beulah, Colorado

Jim Bishop is a man on a mission. Using rocks in the surrounding forest, he started building a one-room stone cottage in 1969 and just never stopped. He now has what he describes as "the largest one-man construction project in the country, quite possibly the world!" Highlights include a tower that ascends high into the sky and a fire-breathing steel dragon that crowns the main structure.

Colorado Gators

Mosca, Colorado

Dubbed the world's only high-altitude alligator farm, Colorado Gators appears a bit out of the place in the Rockies, until you hear of its origins. The proprietors owned a fish farm and bought 100 baby alligators in 1987 to help dispose of waste from the fish. The reptiles thrived and multiplied, basking in the sun on snowbanks above a geothermal lagoon that stays 87 degrees Fahrenheit year-round. The farm has been known to throw an alligator rodeo and even offer gator-wrestling classes.

BRYCE CANYON NATIONAL PARK

Utah

THE NORTHERN SECTION of Bryce Canyon has more hoodoos—rugged spires of rock left behind after erosion—than any other spot in the world. Many of these endless rock towers are shaped like something or someone you've seen in some other place: castles, bridges, towers, presidents, prime ministers, princesses, and even the movie alien E.T.

"It's a hell of a place to lose a cow." EBENEZER BRYCE

32

TEXAS

THE VAST AND VARIED topography of Texas is more diverse than that of most independent countries. There are the desert plains of the Panhandle, the rugged badlands of Trans-Pecos, and the verdant undulations of Hill Country. With all that acreage and variety, the state feels tailor-made for road trips. There's room to roam (77,000 miles of roads), plenty to see, and even more to eat, especially if you like steaks, Tex-Mex, or barbecue.

Big Bend National Park

AMEN

THE BEER CAN HOUSE

Houston

WHAT DO YOU DO with 39,000 beer cans (which, on a six-pack-a-day regimen, took 18 years to save)? You cut off the ends, flatten the sides, and rivet them together to make colorful aluminum siding. That's how John Milkovisch sided his modest home at 222 Malone Street. Fortunately, the motif complemented his yard, which he had already paved over with concrete embedded with marbles and pieces of metal. His wife Mary took it all in stride!

But the hammering Houston sun assailed the siding, overheating the home. So John recycled the lids and pull-tabs, creating curtains, mobiles, and fences, to shade the house. And lower his electric bill.

Imagine it—when the warm Texas winds blow, the whole house becomes a wind chime.

I wouldn't even walk across the street to see this place.

BUILDER JOHN MILKOVISCH

Chinati Foundation

Marfa

This sleepy West Texas ranching town attracts contemporary art aficionados from all over the world to see installations by the late Donald Judd and other avant-garde artists. Located at a former army post, the Chinati Foundation's collection is unusual and thought provoking and includes a giant outdoor horseshoe, barracks containing 100 nearly identical aluminum boxes, and works in such media as paper, smashed cars, and fluorescent light.

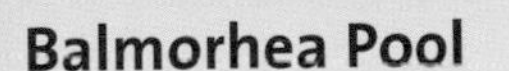

Balmorhea Pool

Balmorhea State Park

There's no antidote for a sweltering summer day like a dip in the pool, especially if it's the world's largest spring-fed swimming pool. Supplied with more than 20 million gallons a day from San Solomon Springs, the 1930s-era pool has a surface area around $1\frac{3}{4}$ acres and a depth of about 25 feet.

Rattlesnake

Freer

Poised to strike visitors to the Freer Chamber of Commerce, this menacing reptilian replica commemorates the Freer Rattlesnake Round-up, an annual festival that began in the 1960s. The event is also dubbed a world's largest (although the folks behind the rattlesnake round-up in Sweetwater, Texas, beg to differ).

Old Rip

Eastland

Built in 1897, the Eastland County Courthouse in northern Texas had a legend living in its cornerstone until the wrecking ball came calling in 1928. Defying all biological explanation, a horned toad somehow lived to see daylight after dwelling in the cornerstone for 31 years. Hoax or not, locals dubbed the reptile "Old Rip" (after Rip Van Winkle) and took him on tour. The famous toad even met President Calvin Coolidge. He passed away soon thereafter and has called the new Eastland County Courthouse home ever since: His embalmed body is on display under glass.

The Big Texan steak ranch

Amarillo

You see the billboards long before the motels lining the Amarillo stretch of I-40 come into sight: "Home of the FREE 72-ounce Steak!!!!" The catch: You've got to finish the whole thing in an hour—or else pay a steep price. Regardless of your appetite, the Big Texan is a bastion of cowboy kitsch, inside and out.

Petrified Wood gas station

Decatur

Proprietor E. F. Boydston put a veneer of locally quarried petrified wood on his gas station to attract customers to his Texas Tourist Camp, which also included a restaurant and rental cabins. It's alleged that long before the gas station closed in 1989, infamous bank robbers Bonnie and Clyde once spent the night in one of the cabins. The place remains a local attraction.

PETRIFIED WOOD STATION
TEXACO
NO GAS
J.R.
TEXAS

The Gulf Coast

AFTER YOU'VE HAD YOUR FILL of the quirky hot spots in and around Houston, hit the road and beat the summer heat at the beaches along the Gulf Coast. A favorite road-trip destination since the advent of the automobile, Padre Island is one of the biggest chunks of undeveloped seashore in the country. The barrier island between mainland Texas and the Gulf of Mexico is a magnet for four-wheel drivers, who love its sandy beaches, as well as boaters, swimmers, and anglers who come for what's just offshore.

Orange Show Monument
AIA Sandcastle Competition
Forbidden Gardens
Padre Island National Seashore
Padre Island
Gulf of Mexico
TEXAS
UNITED STATES
Johnson City
Round Rock
Austin
Navasota
Conroe
Cleveland
Beaumont
Brenham
The Woodlands
Smithville
Lagrange
Hempstead
Houston
Port Arthur
Baytown
Pasadena
New Braunfels
Columbus
Schulenburg
Seguin
Gonzales
Hallettsville
Missouri City
Texas City
San Antonio
Yoakum
Wharton
El Campo
Angleton
Galveston
Cuero
Lake Jackson
Edna
Bay City
Karnes City
Kenedy
Victoria
Goliad
Port Lavaca
Tilden
Beeville
George West
Alice
Corpus Christi
Kingsville
Falfurrias
Edinburg
Harlingen
Ciudad Rio Bravo

FORBIDDEN GARDENS

Katy

BUILT BY A HONG Kong tycoon as a testament to Chinese history, this Houston-area attraction features a one-third scale model of one of China's greatest archaeological finds: Emperor Qin's tomb and its resident army of 6,000 terra-cotta soldiers. The Gardens also include an elaborate model of the Forbidden City.

Congress Avenue Bridge

Austin

At the country's largest urban bat colony, some 1.5 million Mexican free-tailed bats spend their summer days snoozing under Austin's Congress Avenue Bridge. The aerobatic mammals draw a crowd at dusk, then they take off en masse in search of dinner—they eat an estimated 5 to 15 tons of insects per night.

Stats on Bats

- The bats began moving to the Congress Avenue Bridge after a 1980 reconstruction. The deep, narrow spaces under the bridge provided the perfect daytime accommodation for the free-tail bats.

- Austin's bat colony is mostly female—the male bats remain in Mexico (their winter home) while the pregnant females come to Austin. Each bat delivers a single pup early in the summer.

- Late summer is the best time to see spectacular bat flights—just make sure you bring an umbrella!

Great European Cities and Landmarks of North America

FOR THOSE WHO AREN'T too picky, the great European vacation is just a tank of unleaded away. Why hop the pond in pursuit of the sights and sounds of European culture when you can get an Americanized version in your own backyard?

The Globe Theatre
Odessa, Texas

There are two Eiffel Tower replicas in two towns named Paris (one in Texas, one in Tennessee) as well as one in Las Vegas, Nevada, not to mention the Greek Parthenon in Nashville, Tennessee, and the Leaning Tower of Niles, Illinois. The authentic London Bridge is a tourist magnet in Lake Havasu City, Arizona, and a replica of Shakespeare's home stage, the Globe Theatre, is an active venue in Odessa, Texas. Also in Texas: Stonehenge II, aka Stonehenge in the Hills, and the Easter Island statues in Hunt.

Easter Island statues
Hunt, Texas

Eiffel Tower
Paris, Texas

AIA SANDCASTLE COMPETITION

Galveston

SINCE THE MID-1980S, THOUSANDS OF ARCHITECTS and designers have headed to Galveston for the annual American Institute of Architects Sandcastle Competition. Using nothing but sand, water, tools, and hands, contestants have eight hours to craft the sandcastle of their dreams—or just about anything else. The results are impressive and include dragons, mermaids, and happy walruses alongside sandcastles inspired by the Mayans, Romans, Alfred E. Neuman, and J.R.R. Tolkien.

3D/I
PLACE
YOUR
BETS

Big Tex

Dallas

Since 1952, Big Tex has served as the host of the State Fair of Texas. This genial fiberglass cowboy is the tallest in the world at 52 feet—his boots alone are 7 feet tall! Big Tex has undergone several makeovers in the last few decades to fix a "lascivious" wink, straighten his nose, and enable him to talk. He now greets visitors to the fair each year with a hearty "Howdy, folks!"

Ozymandias Leg Ruins

Amarillo

The mind behind Cadillac Ranch—Stanley Marsh 3—has more than one roadside claim to fame in the Amarillo area. The Ozymandias Leg Ruins are another lasting Marsh work: a pair of legs inspired by a Percy Bysshe Shelley poem. The statue's appearance suggests that it was once an entire body (it never was), and a fictional historical marker suggests that students from Lubbock destroyed it.

Everyones Art Car Parade

Houston

Everyones Art Car Parade was inspired by the Fruitmobile, a car decorated for the Orange Show Monument in 1984. The popularity of the Fruitmobile display blossomed into a road show of a few art cars, which in turn grew into Everyones Art Car Parade, featuring more than 250 decorated cars, motorcycles, bikes, and other hard-to-identify wheeled contraptions.

The Orange Show Monument

Houston

The handiwork of postal worker Jefferson Davis McKissack, this east Houston landmark is built of everything from bricks to mannequins to wagon wheels. Sporting an orange-and-white color scheme, the Orange Show is a tribute of sorts to the nutritional value of its creator's favorite fruit—the orange.

HOLD
ON

Killer Bee

Hidalgo

While "Killer Bee Capital of the World" doesn't sound like a moniker that will attract many out-of-towners, Hidalgo has embraced the title and gone a step further by building a 20-foot-long stinger outside city hall. The city nabbed the title after the country's first killer-bee colony was discovered nearby in 1990.

World's Second-largest Fire Hydrant

Beaumont

Painted white with black spots to promote the video release of Disney's *101 Dalmatians,* this 24-foot-tall hydrant was a gift from the studio to the Fire Museum of Texas, where it is on permanent display. The waterworks within the mottled shell actually work, capable of blasting 25 gallons a second. Just two years after the Beaumont hydrant was erected, a 29½-foot-tall fire hydrant was unveiled in Elm Creek, Manitoba, Canada, beating the Beaumont hydrant's "world's largest" status by more than 5 feet.

MUNSTER MANSION

Waxahachie

AS YOU MIGHT GUESS, the owners of this unusual home have a passion for the 1960s television series *The Munsters.* Since November 2001, Charles and Sandra McKee have been building and perfecting their dream house, which replicates as exactly as possible the interior and exterior of the fictional 1313 Mockingbird Lane. Though the mansion is a private residence, it is open for tours once a year during the annual Halloween party.

The Munsters

THE GREAT PLAINS

THE GEOGRAPHIC CENTER of North America is found in Rugby, North Dakota. The entire Great Plains region happens to be the center of one of the continent's densest populations of must-see roadside goliaths. There is a simple philosophy at work here: Big statues are good, but bigger statues are better. Way better!

Hundred-foot-tall likenesses inspire humongous consumer goods for collectors and gatherers who pass through. They are part of the regional culture in the same way skyscrapers are part of New York City. With a bit of ingenuity and elbow grease, a mid-continent town could collectively stake a claim to greatness—in the form of a giant turtle, buffalo, or historical figure.

Mount Rushmore
South Dakota

CARHENGE

Alliance, Nebraska

FOR HIS FAMILY REUNION, engineer Jim Reinders organized a project that became the stuff of legend: the construction of a scale model of Stonehenge using junked American cars instead of slabs of stone. With the help of a backhoe and several cases of beer, Reinders and his kin put together this lasting tribute to a much more mysterious landmark halfway around the world.

"To invent, you need a good imagination and a pile of junk."

THOMAS EDISON

W'eel Turtle

Dunseith, North Dakota

Made from 2,000 tire rims that never made it to their destination, W'eel stands sentinel on the North Dakota prairie and lures customers to Dale's Thrifty Barn, the gas station/café/motel responsible for its existence. The 40-foot turtle's one-ton head bobs from side to side, perhaps acknowledging the surrounding Turtle Mountains or the annual turtle derby in nearby Boissevain, Manitoba.

S. P. Dinsmoor's Garden of Eden

Lucas, Kansas

A Populist, schoolteacher, and veteran of the Civil War, Samuel Perry Dinsmoor started building his log cabin in 1907 out of "limestone timber" because of the lack of trees. Once the cabin was finished, Dinsmoor migrated into the medium of cement and fashioned more than 2,000 sacks of the stuff into his own personal "Garden of Eden," a menagerie of oddly engaging political and religious imagery. The place faded after its creator died in 1932 but was restored in the 1970s and is now listed on the National Register of Historic Places.

Sioux Falls to the Black Hills

THERE ARE FEW STRETCHES of interstate with as many roadside landmarks as this chunk of I-90. Start in Sioux Falls and head west toward Deadwood, taking in the Corn Palace, Wall Drug, and Badlands National Park. A short detour south takes you to the Crazy Horse Memorial and Mount Rushmore, two of the most impressive roadside statues in the world.

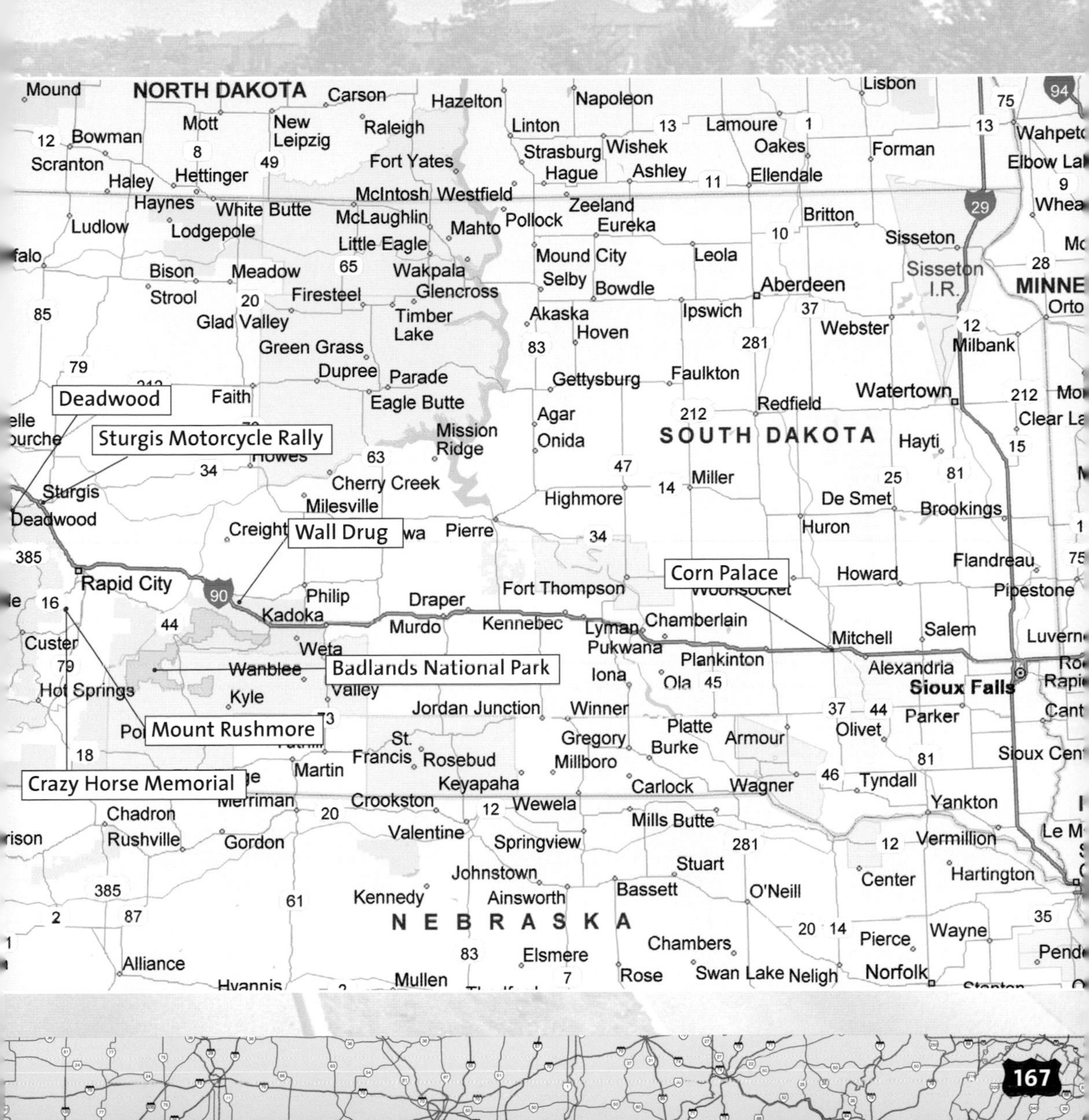
Deadwood
Sturgis Motorcycle Rally
Wall Drug
Corn Palace
Badlands National Park
Mount Rushmore
Crazy Horse Memorial
NORTH DAKOTA
SOUTH DAKOTA
N E B R A S K A
Mound
Carson
Hazelton
Napoleon
Lisbon
Mott
New Leipzig
Raleigh
Linton
Lamoure
Bowman
Scranton
Haley
Hettinger
Fort Yates
Strasburg
Wishek
Oakes
Forman
Hague
Ashley
Ellendale
Haynes
White Butte
McIntosh
Westfield
Zeeland
Ludlow
Lodgepole
McLaughlin
Mahto
Pollock
Eureka
Britton
Sisseton
Little Eagle
Mound City
Leola
Bison
Meadow
Wakpala
Selby
Aberdeen
Sisseton I.R.
Strool
Firesteel
Glencross
Bowdle
Glad Valley
Timber Lake
Akaska
Ipswich
Webster
Hoven
Milbank
Green Grass
Dupree
Parade
Gettysburg
Faulkton
Watertown
Faith
Eagle Butte
Redfield
Mission Ridge
Agar
Onida
Hayti
Clear Lake
Cherry Creek
Miller
Sturgis
Milesville
Highmore
De Smet
Brookings
Huron
Creighton
Pierre
Flandreau
Rapid City
Philip
Fort Thompson
Woonsocket
Howard
Pipestone
Kadoka
Draper
Chamberlain
Murdo
Kennebec
Lyman
Mitchell
Salem
Custer
Weta
Pukwana
Plankinton
Alexandria
Wanblee
Iona
Ola
Sioux Falls
Hot Springs
Kyle
Jordan Junction
Winner
Parker
Platte
Armour
Olivet
St. Francis
Gregory
Burke
Rosebud
Millboro
Martin
Keyapaha
Carlock
Wagner
Tyndall
Merriman
Crookston
Wewela
Yankton
Chadron
Mills Butte
Valentine
Rushville
Gordon
Springview
Vermillion
Stuart
Johnstown
Center
Hartington
Bassett
O'Neill
Kennedy
Ainsworth
Chambers
Pierce
Wayne
Elsmere
Alliance
Rose
Swan Lake
Neligh
Norfolk
Mullen
Hyannis
167

CRAZY HORSE MEMORIAL

Crazy Horse, South Dakota

THE LIFE'S WORK OF Korczak Ziolkowski until his passing in 1982, the Crazy Horse Memorial is likely the most ambitious roadside project ever undertaken. Ziolkowski's mission: to sculpt a 600-foot mountain into the likeness of the legendary warrior on horseback. More than a half-century later, Ziolkowski's family continues his work, but the statue remains very much a work in progress.

"My fellow chiefs and I would like the white man to know that the red man has great heroes, too."

LAKOTA SIOUX CHIEF HENRY STANDING BEAR, IN A 1939 LETTER TO KORCZAK ZIOLKOWSKI

Cow

New Salem, North Dakota

On the edge of I-94, a 38-foot-tall fiberglass Holstein honors the local dairy industry, putting Wisconsin's herds of massive bovines to shame (but it should be noted that it was manufactured in Wisconsin and shipped to North Dakota in three parts). Named "Salem Sue," the big gal is visible from five miles away on its foundation on School Hill.

Buffalo

Jamestown, North Dakota

With dimensions of 26 feet (height) by 46 feet (length) and weighing in at 60 tons, this is a bison that would give ol' Babe the Blue Ox a run for his money. The concrete behemoth stands watch over a prairie that is home to a living, breathing herd managed by the North Dakota Buffalo Foundation.

WALL DRUG STORE

Wall, South Dakota

TED AND DOROTHY HUSTEAD bought the Wall Drug pharmacy in 1931, when the United States was in the throes of the Great Depression. Business was lukewarm for five years until inspiration struck: The couple decided to put up signs advertising free ice water. To spread the word about this and other touristy wiles, the Husteads set up a network of thousands of billboards. And traffic poured in. While one 45-mile segment of I-90 features more than 50 signs, they are not limited to that highway alone. The pharmacy has also advertised in London, Paris, Amsterdam, and Rome. Wall Drug also supplies signs to anyone who wants them, provided they promise to send back a snapshot of the sign on display at its final destination. As a result, photos of signs at the North Pole, the South Pole, and every point in between plaster the drugstore's walls.

A giant fiberglass jackalope stands sentry in the back yard.

All of this advertising has helped the Husteads build an empire that includes not just a drugstore, but also a shopping mall, a 500-seat restaurant, a jackalope (a perfect spot for a photo op), and numerous robots that will gladly perform for a quarter. Today, the place is a sprawling tourist outpost that attracts up to 20,000 visitors on hot summer days, serving some 5,000 glasses of ice water in the process.

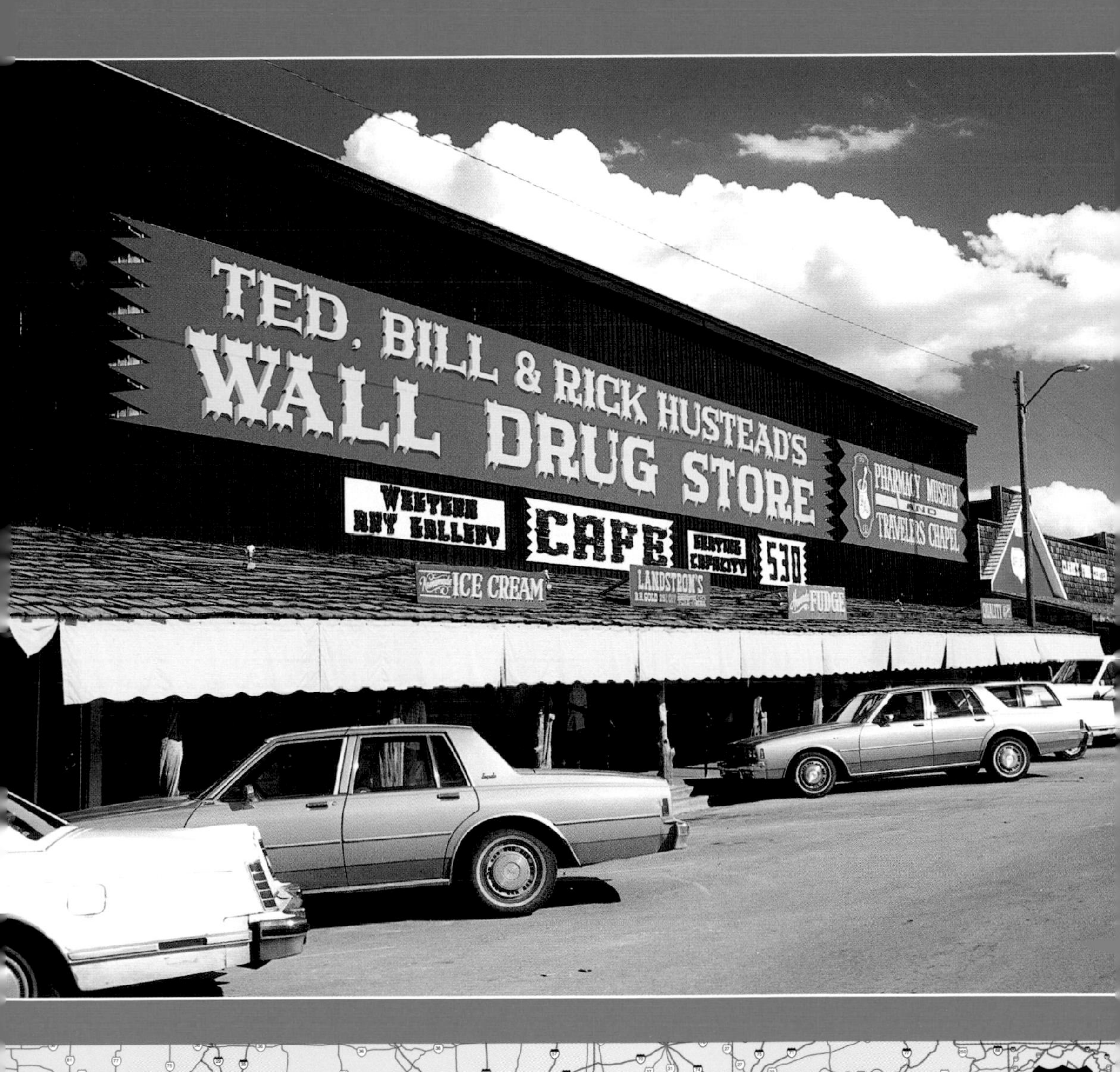
TED, BILL & RICK HUSTEAD'S
WALL DRUG STORE
WESTERN ART GALLERY
CAFE
SEATING CAPACITY
530
PHARMACY MUSEUM
AND
TRAVELERS CHAPEL
ICE CREAM
LANDSTROM'S
FUDGE

DOROTHY'S HOUSE

Liberal, Kansas

"THERE'S NO PLACE like home," chanted *The Wizard of Oz*'s Dorothy Gale as she clicked her ruby slipper–clad heels together. Well, the good folk of Liberal took it upon themselves to designate a house from 1907 as Miss Gale's official residence, and the place now serves as the gateway to an animatronic attraction dubbed the Land of Oz.

"The road to the City of Emeralds is paved with yellow brick."

L. Frank Baum, *The Wonderful Wizard of Oz*

Great American Road-trip Songs

- "On the Road Again," Willie Nelson
- "(Get Your Kicks On) Route 66," Bobby Troup
- "Truckin'," The Grateful Dead
- "I've Been Everywhere," Johnny Cash
- "Ramblin' Man," Allman Brothers Band
- "No Particular Place to Go," Chuck Berry
- "Take Me Home, Country Roads," John Denver
- "Graceland," Paul Simon
- "King of the Road," Roger Miller
- "I Drove All Night," Roy Orbison
- "Roll on Down the Highway," Bachman-Turner Overdrive

Willie Nelson

Johnny Cash

Sturgis Motorcycle Rally

Sturgis, South Dakota

When the biggest motorcycle rally in the United States rolls around each August, this normally sleepy town of 6,000 becomes the biggest temporary city in the state, with a peak population of 500,000. The event has grown tremendously since the first rally was held in 1938 with nine bikers and a small crowd.

THE ENCHANTED HIGHWAY

Hettinger County, North Dakota

THE HIGHEST DENSITY of huge roadside statues might well be North Dakota's Enchanted Highway, a 32-mile stretch of two-lane blacktop that runs between the towns of Gladstone and Regent in Hettinger County. The statues are the handiwork of one Gary Greff, a self-taught sculptor and onetime schoolteacher and principal who feared that Regent would become a ghost town if its economy did not diversify beyond agriculture. So what was Greff's solution to the problem? You've got it—a colony of enormous sculptures on the side of the road.

Deer Crossing (2002)

Greff went to work in the early 1990s and is still at it today. At the time of this writing, the Enchanted Highway was home to seven of Greff's installations: *Tin Family* (1993), *Theodore Roosevelt Rides Again* (1993), *Pheasants on the Prairie* (1996), *Grasshopper's Delight* (1999), *Geese in Flight* (2002), *Deer Crossing* (2002), and *Fisherman's Dream* (2004). Greff also runs the Enchanted Highway Gift Shop in Regent and plans to build several more oversize attractions before he hangs up his welding torch.

Grasshopper's Delight (1999)

Tin Family (1993)

Corn Palace

Mitchell,
South Dakota

Mitchell is the "Corn Capital of the World," a designation backed up by this one-of-a-kind community center. Locals decorate the outside of the turreted, czarist Russia–style palace with murals each year. But there's a twist: The medium is not paint, but thousands of bushels of corn and other South Dakota grains. After the annual fall harvest, pigeons devour the palace's second skin, leaving it to wait out the winter in the buff.

They Also Ran Gallery

Norton, Kansas

The mezzanine of Norton's First State Bank is home to the only museum in the United States dedicated to those who lost presidential elections, with a framed picture and a short biography of each one. The gallery features such famous faces as Thomas Jefferson and John Kerry alongside such lesser-known distinguished losers as General Lewis Cass and Rufus King.

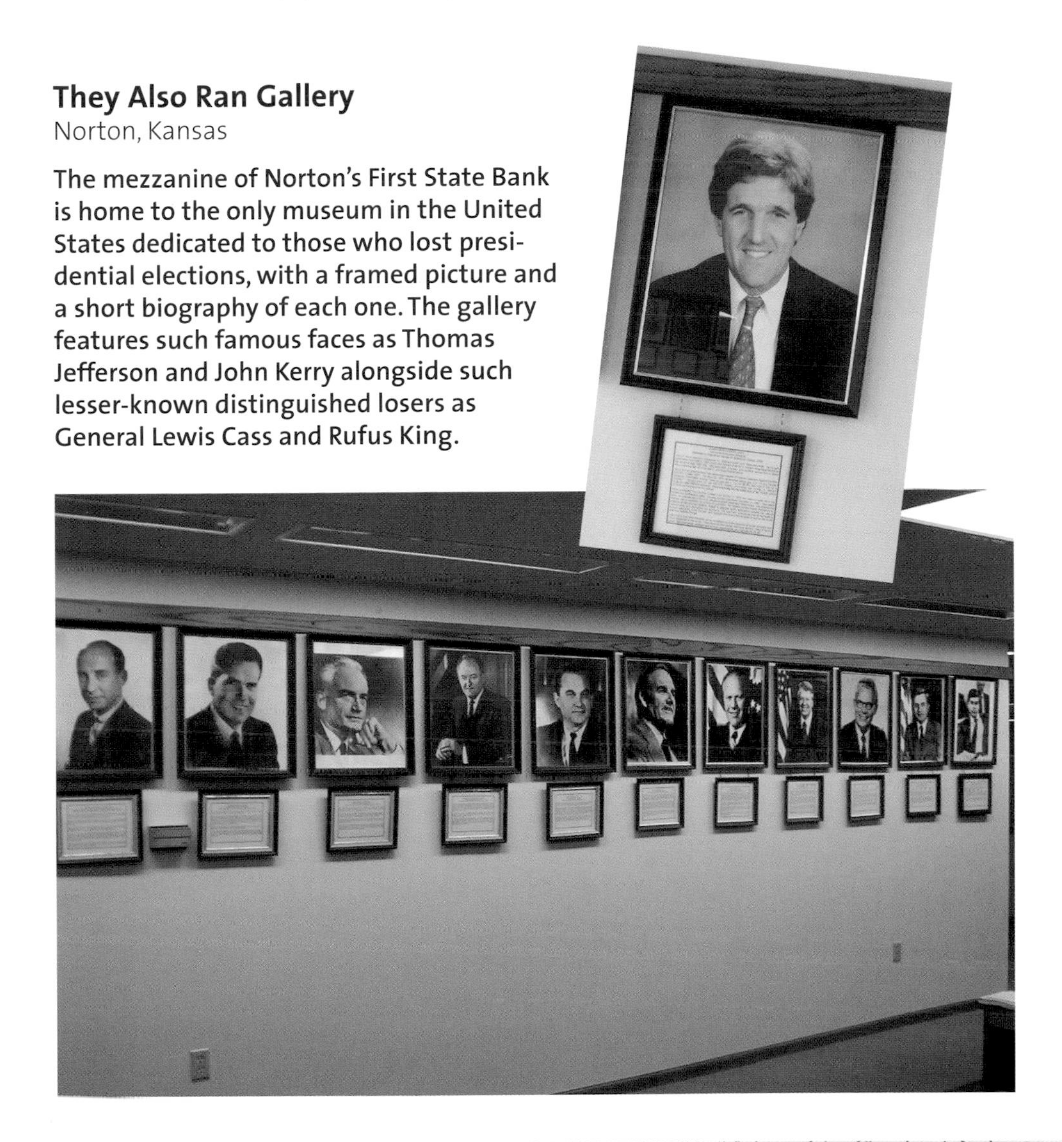

THE MIDWEST

THE HEARTLAND, the nation's breadbasket, and the barometer of mainstream culture—the Midwest is authentic America. For road-trippers, the Midwest's destinations range from the quaint small town to the ultra-cosmopolitan megalopolis, from tallgrass prairieland to the Great Lakes. Cultural diversity is alive in the region's music, from Chicago's blues scene to Detroit's Motown beat to Cleveland's Rock and Roll Hall of Fame. This is also where the road trip was born: Route 66 began in Chicago. And geography puts the region within driving distance of destinations both east and west.

Gateway Arch
St. Louis, Missouri

FOREVERTRON

North Freedom, Wisconsin

DR. EVERMOR (retired junk collector Tom Every) started building the Forevertron in 1983, and the 400-ton curiosity is now considered the world's largest sculpture. Evoking a Victorian view of the far future, Evermor used scrap metal of all kinds to build the monolith with the hope of using it to personally rocket into the cosmos.

Purple Martin Houses

Griggsville, Illinois

Positioned in boggy terrain betwixt the Missouri and Illinois rivers, Griggsville long put up with a serious mosquito infestation until the local Jaycees became wise to the fact that purple martins are the bird world's most prolific skeeter-eaters. To fend off the bugs, they commissioned a manufacturer to make dream homes for the birds. These homes were positioned along Quincy Street, which is now known as Purple Martin Boulevard.

The Spindle

Berwyn, Illinois

In the parking lot of a 1950s-era shopping mall called Cermak Plaza, this oddball work of public art by Los Angeles–based Dustin Shuler features eight automobiles impaled on a 40-foot spike. The mall's proprietor is known for his unusual taste in public art and has commissioned a number of interesting pieces for display at his various retail properties.

1896-1996
BEMIDJI
CENTENNIAL
BEMIDJI
&
PAUL
BUNYAN
1937

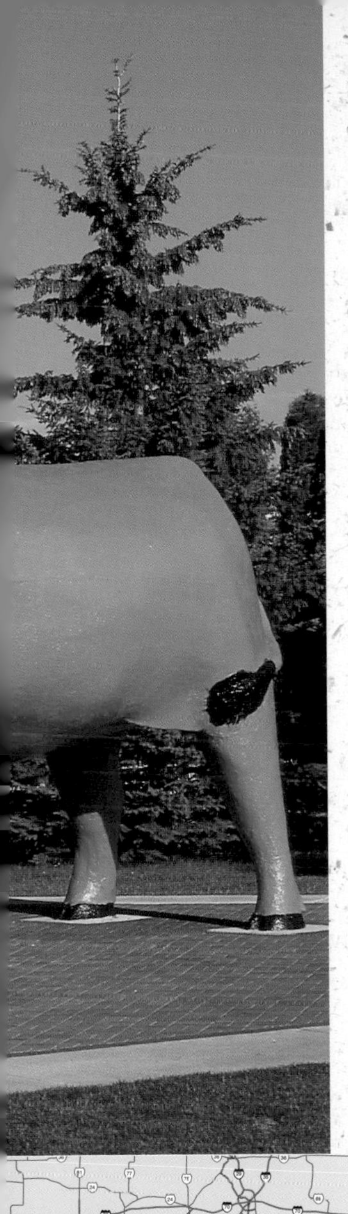

PAUL BUNYAN

Bemidji, Minnesota

BIG PAUL MIGHT JUST be the mascot of the American road. Throughout the northern forests—and almost every other corner of the country—the hero of so many tall tales is immortalized as a gigantic statue, often accompanied by his sidekick, Babe the Blue Ox. The giant lumberjack was said to weigh 80 pounds when five giant storks delivered him as a baby, and he grew so fast he was wearing his father's clothes within a week. He grew up on the coast of Maine but relocated with Babe to Minnesota. The young and rambunctious duo supposedly created the state's 10,000 lakes with their horseplay. Later, Paul went on to invent the logging industry and chop down vast tracts of forest by himself.

Paul's girlfriend, Lucette Diana Kensack, of Hackensack, Minnesota

Mount Horeb Mustard Museum

Mount Horeb, Wisconsin

Depressed over the Boston Red Sox losing the World Series in 1986, Barry Levensen found solace in an unusual place: the mustard display of an all-night grocery store. He resolved to amass the world's largest collection of mustard and opened the museum in 1992. The Mustard Museum now displays more than 4,100 mustards, along with mustard-related memorabilia such as antique mustard pots and mustard advertisements.

Great American Culinary Destinations

- Washington Banana Museum, Auburn, Washington
- Ben & Jerry's Ice Cream Factory, Waterbury, Vermont
- Hershey's Chocolate World, Hershey, Pennsylvania
- Colonel Sanders Cafe and Museum, Corbin, Kentucky
- Mount Horeb Mustard Museum, Mount Horeb, Wisconsin
- Kellogg's Cereal City USA, Battle Creek, Michigan
- Easton Museum of Pez Dispensers, Easton, Pennsylvania
- Culinary Archives and Museum, Johnson and Wales University, Providence, Rhode Island
- Idaho Potato Expo, Blackfoot, Idaho

Mount Horeb Mustard Museum

Ball of Paint

Alexandria, Indiana

In 1977, local resident Mike Carmichael started applying layer after layer of paint to an ordinary baseball. Since then, the ball has seen an average of two coats a day, earning the title "The World's Largest Ball of Paint." After more than 20,000 coats, the ball measures about three feet in diameter and weighs well over 1,300 pounds.

Bull

Audubon, Iowa

Named after local banker Albert Kruse, Albert the Bull is 45 tons of concrete Hereford. He was built as a monument to Operation T-Bone Days, an event held annually in September when local cattle board the train to the Chicago stockyards. An interesting note: The bull's internal steel frame is made from dismantled Iowa windmills.

Wisconsin Kitsch Tour

TAKE A SPIN NORTH on I-94 from the Windy City into the wacky countryside of America's Dairyland. With attractions like House On the Rock and Forevertron, road trips don't get any stranger than this.

Cloudgate
Chicago, Illinois

Forevertron
House On The Rock
Mount Horeb Mustard Museum
Wrigley Field
The Spindle
Cloudgate
WISCONSIN
UNITED STATES
ILLINOIS
INDIANA
Lake Michigan
Green Bay
Appleton
Neenah
Oshkosh
Fond du Lac
Sheboygan
Manitowoc
Two Rivers
Kewaunee
Sturgeon Bay
Shawano
Marshfield
Stevens Point
Wisconsin Rapids
Plover
Waupaca
Wautoma
Friendship
Mauston
Tomah
Montello
Waupun
Reedsburg
Portage
Beaver Dam
West Bend
Richland Center
Watertown
Madison
West Allis
Milwaukee
Dodgeville
Lancaster
Darlington
Monroe
Janesville
Racine
Kenosha
Galena
Waukegan
Crystal Lake
Freeport
Rockford
Belvidere
Elgin
Schaumburg
Chicago
Mount Carroll
De Kalb
Clinton
Morrison
Dixon
Sterling
Aurora
Naperville
Davenport
Moline
Mendota
Kewanee
Streator
Kankakee
Galesburg
Monmouth
Pontiac
Watseka
Michigan City
Gary
La Porte
Valparaiso
South Bend
Elkhart
Goshen
Plymouth
Rochester
Winamac
Rensselaer
Logansport
Manistee
Ludington
Baldwin
White Cloud
Muskegon
Norton Shores
Grand Haven
Holland
Kalamazoo
St. Joseph
Beulah

Gemini Giant

Wilmington, Illinois

A converted Muffler Man beckons passersby on what was once Route 66 to stop for a burger and a soda at the Launching Pad Drive-in. The big guy was given a space-age spin with his chrome helmet and rocket in hand, in hopes of causing future hungry travelers to put on the brakes.

Superman

Metropolis, Illinois

Metropolis, Illinois, with a population of 15,000 (including the city and the county), is not quite the Metropolis of DC Comics fame. But it predates Superman by a long shot, as it was founded in 1839. In 1972, the town decided to capitalize on the association and adopted the "Hometown of Superman" moniker. A seven-foot statue went up in 1986, only to be replaced seven years later by this more impressive 15-foot bronze. The town is also home to a Superman museum and plays host to a Superman festival in June.

Longaberger building

Newark, Ohio

The world headquarters of the Longaberger Basket Company is an exact replica of one of the company's baskets—except for the fact that this one is 160 times larger and cost $30 million to build. Large windows are strategically located within the seven-story basket's weave, and the upright handles each weigh 75 tons.

Jolly Green Giant

Blue Earth,
Minnesota

Ho, ho, ho—Green Giant! Wearing a size 78 shoe, this 55-foot-tall likeness pays homage to the third-most recognizable advertising icon of the 20th century. The statue's geographical significance: The Green Giant Company began in the fertile farmland that surrounds Blue Earth.

Kansas City Sculpture Park

Kansas City, Missouri

THIS 22-ACRE PARK IS HOME to a large collection of modern outdoor sculptures, including *30 Standing Bronze Figures* by Magdalena Abakanowicz (above) and *Shuttlecocks,* a set of four 18-foot-tall badminton "birdies" by artists Claes Oldenburg and Coosje van Bruggen (right). The sculpture park is part of the Nelson-Atkins Museum of Art, which serves as the "net" over which the giant shuttlecocks appear to have been swatted.

"Sculpture is the art of the intelligence."

Pablo Picasso

Virginia, Minnesota

WHICH IS LOONIER?

TETHERED IN THE MIDDLE of Silver Lake in Virginia, Minnesota, by an unseen underwater chain, this 21-foot-long loon has been dubbed by locals as the world's largest loon decoy.

Mercer, Wisconsin, the self-titled "Loon Capital of the World," is home to a 16-foot loon that weighs a ton and is said to be the world's largest talking loon (when it's working).

Mercer, Wisconsin

Fred Smith's Wisconsin Concrete Park

Phillips, Wisconsin

Tavern proprietor and retired logger Fred Smith has worked in the traditional folk art medium of concrete and broken glass to document the Wisconsin lifestyle of the early 20th century. The product is an eye-catching park that bears his name and is populated with 250 of his creations, including likenesses of people (lumberjacks, hunters) and animals (deer, moose, bears).

Wegner Grotto

Cataract, Wisconsin

German immigrants Paul and Matilda Wegner spent nearly all of the 1930s dressing up their farm with concrete, glass, and crockery. Their creations include a giant wedding cake, an ocean liner, and a small chapel.

House on the Rock

Spring Green, Wisconsin

CAPPING A 60-FOOT geological formation named Deer Shelter Rock is one of the best-known architectural oddities in the United States. The House on the Rock (a parody of Frank Lloyd Wright's work) is the creation of Alex Jordan, who started building it in the 1940s as a vacation home near Spring Green. He just kept on building, furnishing it with art, a three-story bookcase, and anything else that captured his fevered imagination. He soon realized the place could lure tourists by the carload and started charging 50 cents for tours. Jordan sold the house in the late 1980s, but the place just keeps getting bigger and stranger by the year. With 14 unique

and lavishly decorated rooms—including the Infinity Room, with 3,264 windows—and a surrounding complex that houses a miniature circus, the world's largest carousel, and a full-fledged destination resort, the House on the Rock is at once wacky, tacky, innovative, and elegant.

Tire

Allen Park, Michigan

The 80-foot Uniroyal Tire was first a Ferris wheel at the New York 1964–65 World's Fair before its creators brought it back home to Michigan. While it would fit on a 200-foot-tall car just fine, today the 12-ton radial serves as an advertisement at Uniroyal headquarters just off I-94.

Cuckoo Clock

Wilmot, Ohio

One of many tourist magnets at the Swiss-theme Alpine Homestead Restaurant, this intricate 23½-foot-tall cuckoo clock has been in heated competition with the Bavarian Clock Haus in Frankenmuth, Michigan, for the title. (Wilmot supporters argue that a house can't be considered a true clock.) The place is also a cheese factory.

Cedar Point

Sandusky, Ohio

One of the oldest, biggest, and most popular amusement parks in the country, Cedar Point has been an innovator in the amusement business since 1870. A paradise for thrill seekers, Cedar Point features 16 roller coasters among its 68 rides. At 420 feet and reaching speeds up to 120 miles per hour, the Top Thrill Dragster is one of the tallest and fastest roller coasters in the world.

Great American Amusement Parks

Holiday World

- Holiday World, Santa Claus, Indiana
- Disneyland, Anaheim, California
- Big Chief's Kart and Coaster World, Wisconsin Dells, Wisconsin
- Dollywood, Pigeon Forge, Tennessee
- Walt Disney World, Orlando, Florida
- Lake Compounce Amusement Park, Bristol, Connecticut
- Santa Cruz Beach Boardwalk, Santa Cruz, California
- Six Flags Great Adventure, Jackson, New Jersey
- Busch Gardens, Tampa, Florida
- Silver Dollar City, Branson, Missouri
- Sesame Place, Langhorne, Pennsylvania

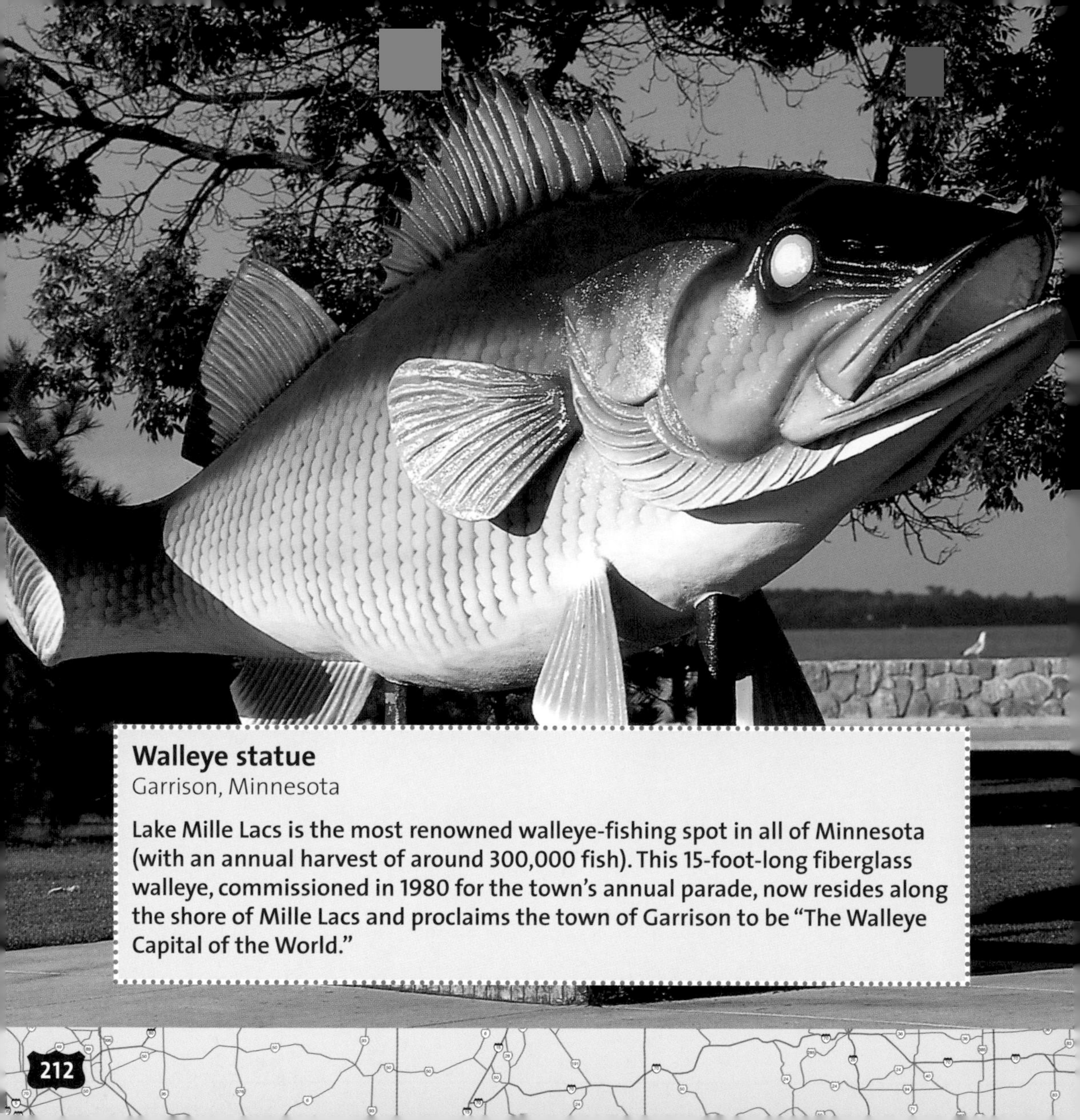

Walleye statue

Garrison, Minnesota

Lake Mille Lacs is the most renowned walleye-fishing spot in all of Minnesota (with an annual harvest of around 300,000 fish). This 15-foot-long fiberglass walleye, commissioned in 1980 for the town's annual parade, now resides along the shore of Mille Lacs and proclaims the town of Garrison to be "The Walleye Capital of the World."

Really Big Fish

Hayward, Wisconsin

The centerpiece of the National Fresh Water Fishing Hall of Fame, these fish are so big there's no need for exaggeration. From tip to tail, the concrete, steel, and fiberglass muskie (right) is 140 feet in length and 4 ½ stories tall. There's a museum in its belly, and its toothy maw doubles as an observation platform.

Praying Hands Memorial

Webb City, Missouri

These disembodied clasped hands burst out of a hill in Webb City's King Jack Park, suggesting a much larger statue in the ground below. Local artist Jack Dawson created the 32-foot steel-and-stucco monument to the power of prayer when he was 20 years old.

"A good traveler has no fixed plans,
and is not intent on arriving."

Lao Tzu

LOVELAND CASTLE

Loveland, Ohio

IN 1929, HARRY ANDREWS FORMED a Boy Scout troop called the Knights of the Golden Trail. The next logical step was to build a castle, which he did single-handedly over the next 50 years. The result is a 17-room full-scale replica of a medieval castle (except for the ballroom, which is 1/5-scale). Originally named Chateau Laroche ("Rock Castle"), the castle was built using local river rocks.

The castle contains a banquet hall, an armory, a chapel, and of course, a dungeon. Today, the Knights of the Golden Trail maintain the castle and offer tours and overnight stays.

CHATEAU LAROCHE

THE MID-ATLANTIC

THE POPULATION CENTER of the country, the Mid-Atlantic makes urban living an art form in its sprawling cities. Dubbed "Skyscraper National Park" by writer Kurt Vonnegut, New York City is one of the top tourist draws in the world, attracting nearly 40 million visitors each year.

Outside of all the big, vertical cities, there is plenty to do. Time-honed means for getting away from it all include regional destinations such as New York's Catskill Mountains, Maryland's Assateague Island, and the New Jersey Shore. Road-trippers can exercise their odometers and get a good dose of nostalgia at Maryland's American Dime Museum, Pennsylvania's Roadside America, and New York's Coney Island.

New York City

HOUDINI MUSEUM
Scranton, Pennsylvania

ESCAPE ARTIST AND MAGICIAN extraordinaire Harry Houdini performed regularly in Scranton. To celebrate his life and legendary career, the Houdini Museum displays milk jugs, strait-jackets, and the handcuffs the magician used in his daring escapes. And no tour would be complete without a magic show. The Houdini Museum also hosts a Houdini Séance each Halloween.

"My brain is the key that sets me free."

HARRY HOUDINI

Big Duck

Flanders, New York

Conceived by "duck rancher" Martin Maurer and his wife, Jeule, as a means of selling the Peking ducks they raised, Long Island's Big Duck was built in Riverhead and relocated to Flanders in 1936. After development threatened the Big Duck in 1987, the owners donated the building to Suffolk County, and it was relocated to a park, where it now serves as a gift shop and tourist information center.

"The rewards of the journey far outweigh the risk of leaving the harbor."
UNKNOWN

Herschell Carrousel Factory Museum

North Tonawanda, New York

Carousels manufactured in Allan Herschell–owned companies account for nearly half of the hand-carved, antique, wooden carousels in existence in North America today. Exhibits in the factory museum walk visitors through the craft of carousel-making, and a pair of vintage carousels allow visitors of all ages to enjoy a ride to yesteryear.

Original American Kazoo Company Factory and Museum

Eden, New York

The Original American Kazoo Company began cranking out kazoos in 1916 and is now the only metal kazoo maker in the world. Visitors can view the entire kazoo-making process, with the original factory equipment, at the museum. Displays include rarified silver and gold kazoos, as well as kazoos of different shapes and sizes. A big metal kazoo—said to be the world's largest—is on the roof.

ROADSIDE AMERICA

Shartlesville, Pennsylvania

THE WORLD'S LARGEST miniature village, Roadside America is the product of decades of painstaking labor by carpenter Laurence Gieringer. The village includes hundreds of miniature buildings, waterways, people, and trains. There's a working flour mill, an underground coal mine, and 10,000 miniature handmade trees in the attraction, which has been a tourist draw in Pennsylvania Dutch Country since the 1930s.

Fairfield at Dawn

Moon over Roadside America

The Shrine Church

Saw Mill on the Hill

Jersey Shore

From Sandy Hook to Cape May, the New Jersey Shore has been a road-trip mecca for a long time: In 1870, Atlantic City unveiled the world's first beachfront boardwalk. Local dignitaries continue to usher in tourist season when they "unlock" the Atlantic Ocean every Memorial Day weekend, as they have since the early 20th century. From Lucy the Elephant at the Margate beach to the Miss Crustacean Pageant in Ocean City, there is no shortage of kooky destinations still going strong today.

Lucy the Elephant

Margate, New Jersey

Looming 65 feet over the Margate beach, Lucy the Elephant is the only example of "zoomorphic architecture" left in the United States, with staircases in her legs leading to rooms inside. The big girl was originally built as a real estate promotion, and she has since served as summer home, tavern, hotel, and tourist attraction. A 1970 relocation spared Lucy from the wrecking ball; preservationists completed a loving restoration in 2000.

American Dime Museum

Baltimore, Maryland

BEFORE THE ARRIVAL OF the traveling sideshow, the dime museum was one of the pillars of the 19th century entertainment industry in the United States, putting hoaxes and oddities on display and charging a dime for a peek. The American Dime Museum re-creates this colorful history with an unusual collection that includes Amazonian mummies, five-pawed dogs, a big ball of rubber bands, feathered fish, and shrunken heads. Some are real, some are not, and the distinction is usually obvious.

MELVIN
WONDER

Haines Shoe House

York, Pennsylvania

Mahlon Haines was a shoe tycoon who made his fortune with the help of creative advertising. His most visible legacy sits on the side of Route 30: a two-story, three-bedroom house shaped like a shoe, complete with a shoe-shape doghouse out back. Once loaned out to newlyweds and elderly couples, Haines Shoe House is now a bed-and-breakfast. Today, anyone with money to spare can shoehorn themselves into the house for a stay.

"We may run, walk, stumble, drive, or fly, but let us never lose sight of the reason for the journey, or miss a chance to see a rainbow on the way."

ANONYMOUS

Niagara Falls

The National Road

THE ORIGINAL TRANSCONTINENTAL HIGHWAY begins in Baltimore and works its way through Pennsylvania after a quick swing through West Virginia. Chocolate fans can make a detour to Hershey, and roller-coaster enthusiasts will enjoy a side trip to Altoona, home of the world's oldest coaster.

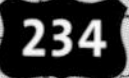

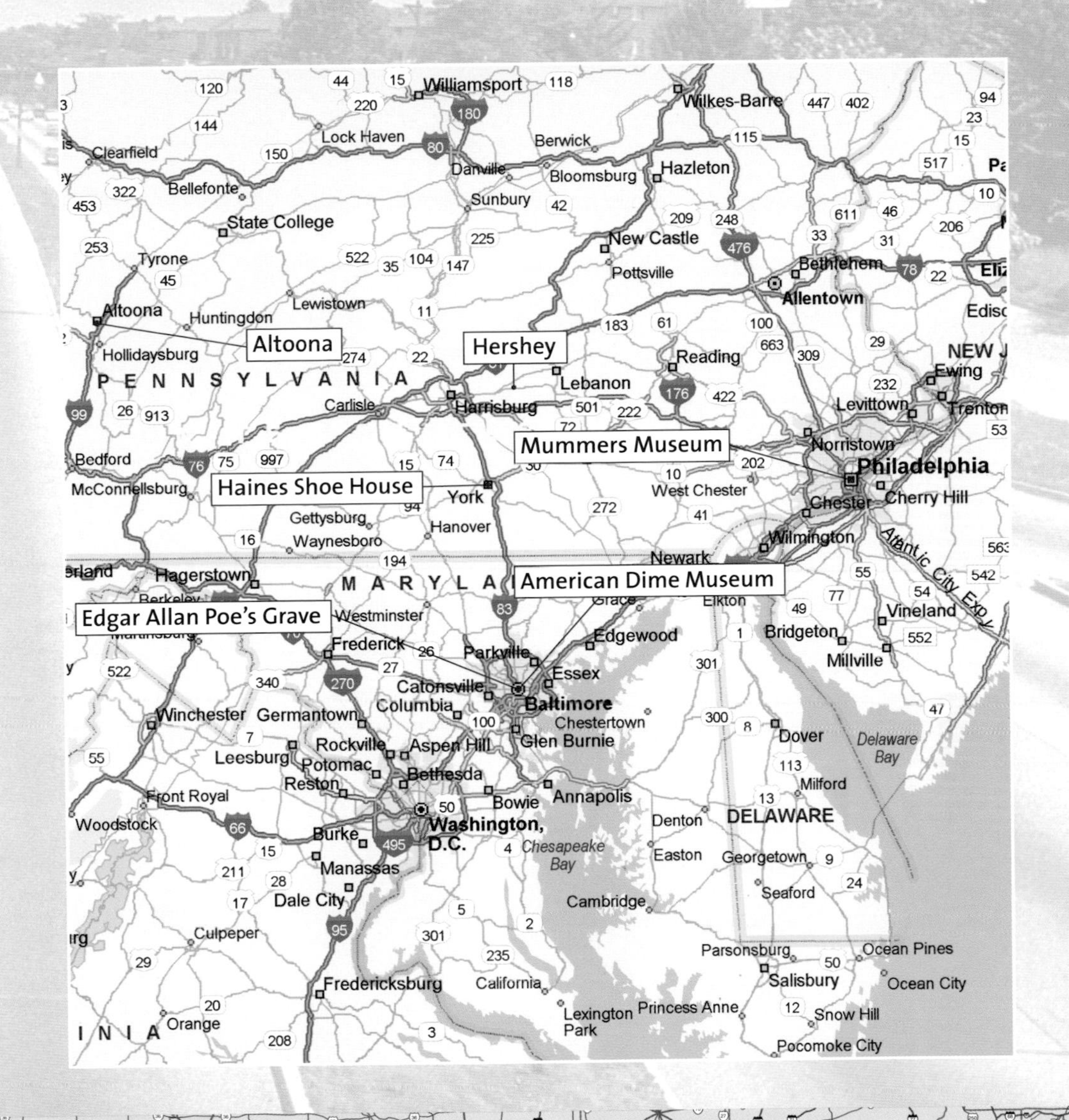

Altoona
Hershey
Mummers Museum
Haines Shoe House
American Dime Museum
Edgar Allan Poe's Grave
PENNSYLVANIA
MARYLA
DELAWARE
Williamsport
Wilkes-Barre
Clearfield
Lock Haven
Berwick
Hazleton
Danville
Bloomsburg
Bellefonte
Sunbury
State College
New Castle
Pottsville
Bethlehem
Allentown
Tyrone
Lewistown
Huntingdon
Hollidaysburg
Reading
Lebanon
NEW J
Ewing
Carlisle
Harrisburg
Levittown
Trenton
Norristown
Philadelphia
Bedford
McConnellsburg
York
West Chester
Cherry Hill
Chester
Gettysburg
Hanover
Waynesboro
Wilmington
Newark
Hagerstown
Elkton
Westminster
Vineland
Frederick
Bridgeton
Parkville
Edgewood
Millville
Essex
Catonsville
Baltimore
Columbia
Winchester
Germantown
Chestertown
Dover
Rockville
Aspen Hill
Glen Burnie
Delaware Bay
Leesburg
Potomac
Bethesda
Reston
Milford
Front Royal
Bowie
Annapolis
Woodstock
Washington, D.C.
Denton
Burke
Easton
Georgetown
Chesapeake Bay
Manassas
Seaford
Dale City
Cambridge
Culpeper
Parsonsburg
Ocean Pines
Salisbury
Ocean City
Fredericksburg
California
Lexington Park
Princess Anne
Snow Hill
Orange
Pocomoke City
Atlantic City Expy

FALLINGWATER

Bear Run, Pennsylvania

THIS THREE-LEVEL HOME was designed by Frank Lloyd Wright for the family of Pittsburgh department store owner Edgar J. Kaufmann in 1936. The family wanted the house, which was used as a guest house and family getaway, to be near the waterfall on their property. Wright took the idea one step further and built the house directly above the waterfall, integrating it with the natural surroundings by mimicking the natural ledges of the waterfall and using local sandstone in the building's construction. The interior furnishings and light fixtures were designed by Wright as well.

"An architect's most useful tools are an eraser at the drafting board, and a wrecking bar at the site."

FRANK LLOYD WRIGHT

CONEY ISLAND

Brooklyn, New York

CONEY ISLAND HAS BEEN New York's playground since the 1800s. Entertainment barons built such famed amusement parks as Dreamland and Luna Park here in the early 20th century. The parks thrived until the onset of the Great Depression brought an onslaught of inexpensive sideshow acts and midway games.

In the shadows cast by legendary roller coasters like the Cyclone—a National Historic Landmark that's been rolling since 1927—Coney Island's sideshow heritage lives on at Sideshows by the Seashore, a performance venue and vocational school. The Coney Island Museum preserves everything else, from souvenir cups to fun-house mirrors. Summertime events run the gamut from the gloriously odd Mermaid Parade, a moving aquatic-themed art gallery, to Nathan's Famous Hot Dog Eating Contest.

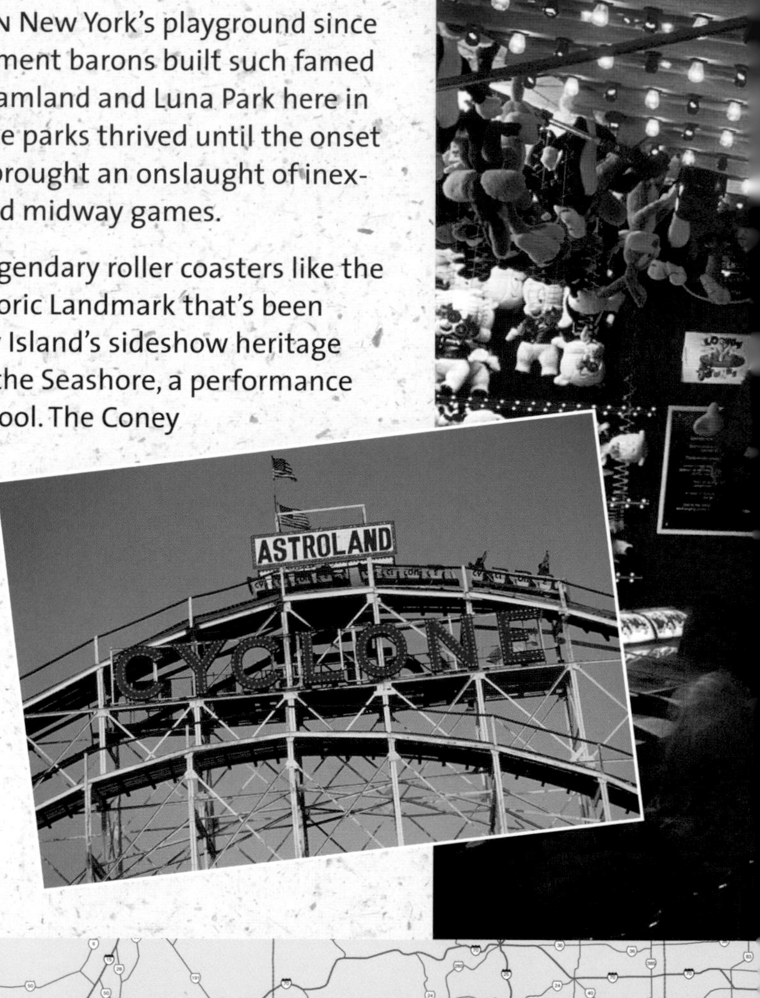

"Coney Island, between June and September, is the world." GEORGE C. TILYOU

George Washington's Bathtub

Berkeley Springs, West Virginia

George Washington often visited Berkeley Springs to avail himself of the "healing" mineral baths fed by the area's natural warm springs. Each spring the town honors this heritage with George Washington's Bathtub Celebration. Washington-themed events include a period dinner, readings from his diary entries, and of course, visits to "the only outdoor monument to presidential bathing."

Great American Haunted Places

- Edgar Allan Poe's Grave, Baltimore, Maryland
- Historic Voodoo Museum, New Orleans, Louisiana
- Salem Witch Museum, Salem, Massachusetts
- Sleepy Hollow Bridge, Sleepy Hollow, New York
- St. Simons Island Lighthouse, St. Simons Island, Georgia
- *St. Peter* Shipwreck, Pultneyville, New York
- Belcourt Castle, Newport, Rhode Island
- Shanghai Tunnels, Portland, Oregon
- Harbor Inn, Traverse City, Michigan

Edgar Allan Poe's Grave

"Those who dream by day are cognizant of many things which escape those who dream only by night."

EDGAR ALLAN POE

BALLET

MUMMERS PARADE AND MUSEUM

Philadelphia, Pennsylvania

THE TRADITION OF MUMMERY dates back to the ancient Roman ritual of Saturnalia, a day of gift exchange and satirical performance that included a parade of laborers wearing masks. Mummery is taken very seriously in Philadelphia. Dozens of Mummers clubs work all year, devising outlandish clown makeup and garish costumes to be worn on the annual New Year's Day parade, in which some 15,000 Mummers participate. Although the parade struts through Philly just once a year, visitors can explore the Mummers Museum year-round.

PRABHUPADA'S PALACE OF GOLD

New Vrindaban, West Virginia

THIS IS THE FORMER temple of the late Srila Prabhupada, who spread the philosophy of Krishna consciousness through the West after leaving his native India in 1965. He first stayed in a shack in New Vrindaban in 1969, and his followers later spent seven years building this magnificent golden palace.

OPUS 40

Saugerties, New York

INSPIRED BY AN ANCIENT Mayan sculpture in Honduras, sculptor Harvey Fite spent the final 37 years of his life creating Opus 40. In 1938 he purchased an abandoned bluestone quarry and began to shape the land using traditional quarrying methods. Fite's monumental project interlocks terraces, ramps, fountains, and statues with the Catskills landscape. Fite used no mortar or cement in the creation of Opus 40; rather, he used a technique known as "dry keying" to carefully fit the stones together.

NEW ENGLAND

In a historical sense, New England is the nation's launching pad. In 1620 the Pilgrims landed at Plymouth Rock in what is now Massachusetts and established the first permanent European settlement in New England. Later came the first university, the first park, the first lighthouse, the first newspaper, and the first pink flamingo (you can thank Worcester, Massachusetts, for that).

Rich in history, cuisine, and quirky museums, New England was an endpoint for the Pilgrims and a starting point for the nation, and it fits the bill as either for today's road-tripper. Thanks to an assortment of attractions encompassing bad art, thirsty frogs, and a house made of newspaper, there's plenty of distraction along winding roads.

Boston Harbor

Barnum Museum

Bridgeport, Connecticut

THE HOST OF THE "Greatest Show on Earth," P. T. Barnum, lived in Bridgeport for much of his adult life and was even elected its mayor in 1855. This makes the city a natural setting for the Barnum Museum, which illuminates his storied life and career. Exhibits include a miniature circus; personal effects of General Tom Thumb (Barnum's most famous act), including a slice of his wedding cake; and a reproduction of the phony Feejee Mermaid, one of many shams Barnum perpetuated on an unsuspecting public.

Skeleton of Jumbo, a famous 19th century Barnum circus elephant

"Every crowd has a silver lining."

P. T. BARNUM

Jack Kerouac Commemorative and Park

Lowell, Massachusetts

Before he wrote *On the Road*, Jack Kerouac spent his formative years in Lowell. The nomadic scribe is honored in his hometown by a monument in an eponymous park that includes excerpts from his novels as well as Roman Catholic and Buddhist symbols that reflect the late writer's diverse beliefs.

Great American Road-trip Books

- *On the Road,* Jack Kerouac
- *Blue Highways: A Journey into America,* William Least Heat-Moon
- *Travels with Charley: In Search of America,* John Steinbeck

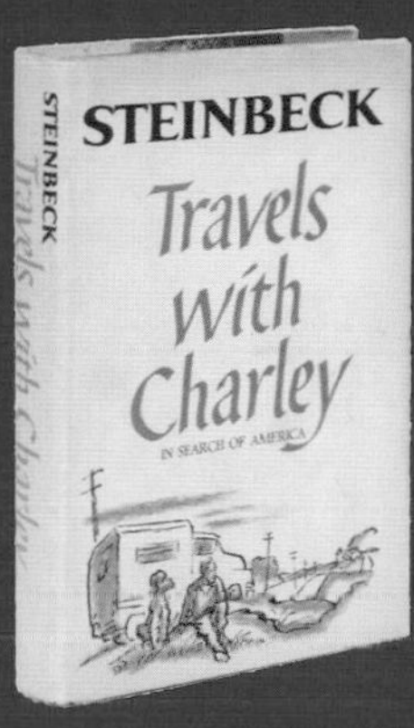

- *The Electric Kool-Aid Acid Test,* Tom Wolfe

- *Roads: Driving America's Great Highways,* Larry McMurtry

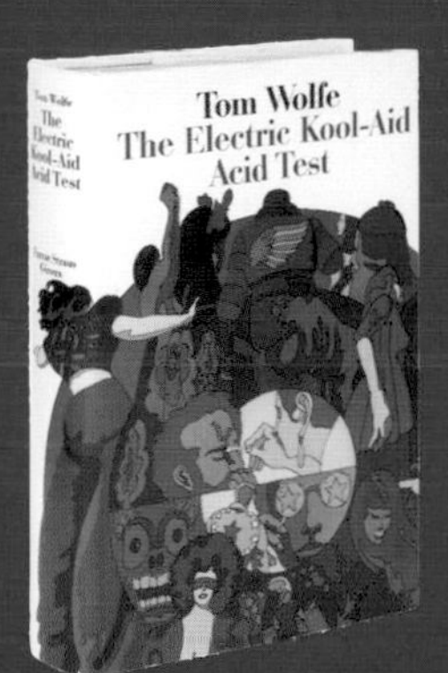

- *Zen and the Art of Motorcycle Maintenance,* Robert Pirsig
- *The Lost Continent: Travels in Small-Town America,* Bill Bryson

BEN & JERRY'S FACTORY

Waterbury, Vermont

IN 1978, childhood friends Ben Cohen and Jerry Greenfield converted a gas station in Burlington into the first Ben & Jerry's store and began making "Vermont's Finest" ice cream. Over the years, the company has expanded nationally and internationally while keeping its commitment to be friendly to the community and to the environment—Ben & Jerry's uses non-bleached paperboard to hold their tasty pints. Tours of the factory include a movie, a first-hand look at the ice cream making process, and of course, mouth-watering samples of the flavors of the day.

Flavors that are retired from the Ben & Jerry's lineup rest in peace in the Flavor Graveyard.

Top Ten Ben & Jerry's Flavors

1. Cherry Garcia® Ice Cream
2. Chocolate Chip Cookie Dough Ice Cream
3. Chunky Monkey® Ice Cream
4. Chocolate Fudge Brownie™ Ice Cream
5. Half Baked™ Ice Cream
6. Phish Food® Ice Cream
7. Cherry Garcia® Low Fat Frozen Yogurt
8. New York Super Fudge Chunk® Ice Cream
9. Peanut Butter Cup™ Ice Cream
10. Vanilla Ice Cream

GILLETTE CASTLE

East Haddam, Connecticut

GILLETTE CASTLE WAS THE home of William Hooker Gillette, a noted stage actor and director who designed the medieval-looking structure himself. It took a team of 20 laborers a full five years to complete the 24-room castle, made from local fieldstone and reinforced with steel. Now a state park, the place is chock full of eccentricities: a table that slides on tracks, couches carved into the stone, and a three-mile railroad (complete with a "Grand Central" station) encircling the grounds.

Frog Bridge

Willimantic, Connecticut

This whimsical bridge pays tribute to two disparate phenomena. The spools are monuments to the thread industry that was the backbone of the local economy in the 19th century. The frogs perched atop the spools are reminders of the infamous "Battle of the Frogs" of 1754, when the cries from dying, drought-ravaged bullfrogs seriously alarmed locals during the thick of the French and Indian War.

"What is the feeling when you're driving away from people, and they recede on the plain till you see their specks dispersing? —it's the too huge world vaulting us, and it's good—bye. But we lean forward to the next crazy venture beneath the skies."

JACK KEROUAC, *ON THE ROAD*

Boston to Acadia National Park

ALL SORTS OF INTRIGUING attractions dot this route, beginning with those in the nooks and crannies of Beantown, continuing up the New England coast into the realm of witches and mammoth lobsters, and ending in the sublime surroundings of Acadia National Park.

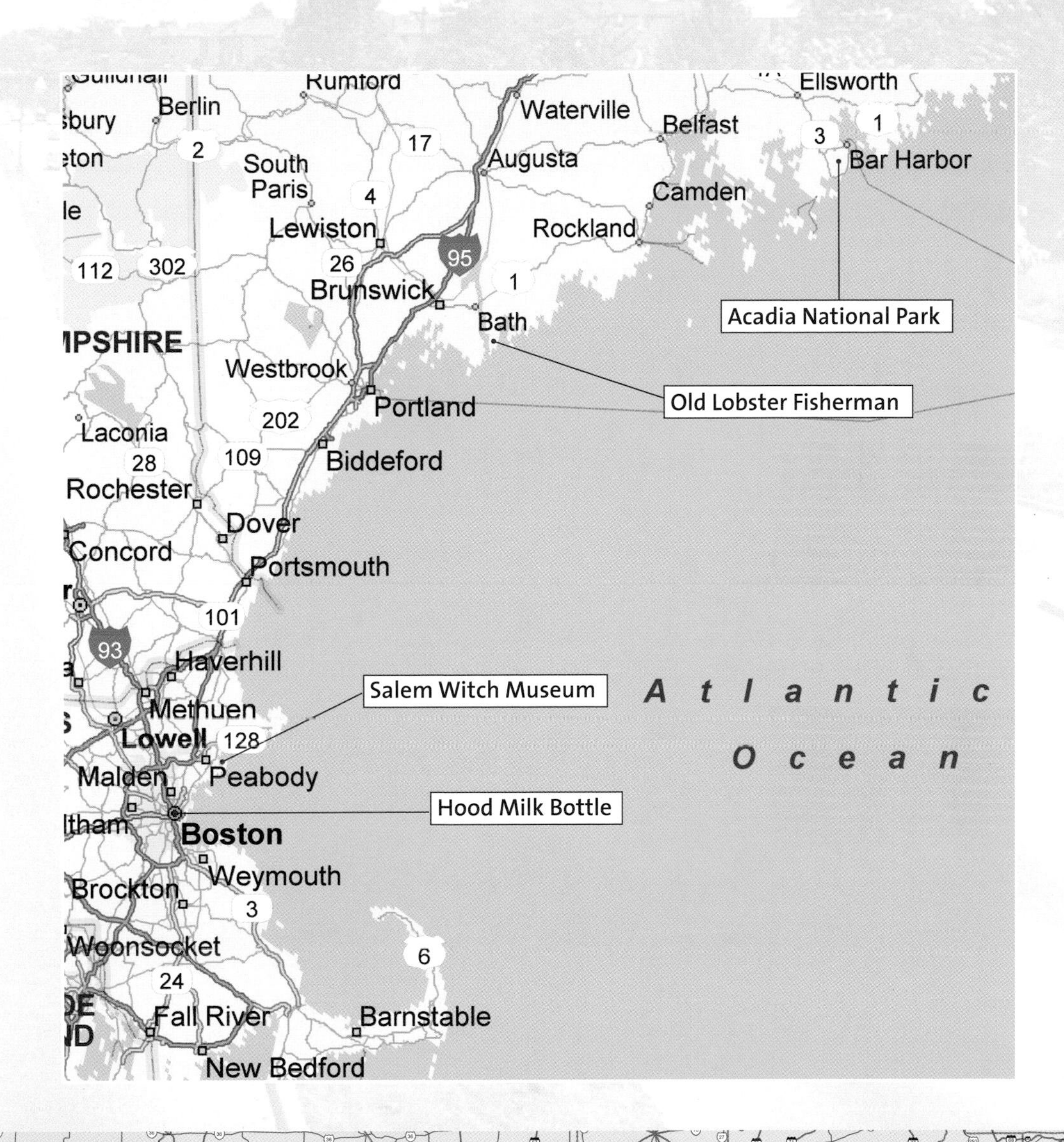

Rumford
Ellsworth
Berlin
Waterville
Belfast
1
3
Bar Harbor
2
17
South
Paris
Augusta
4
Camden
Lewiston
Rockland
95
112
302
26
1
Brunswick
Bath
Acadia National Park
Westbrook
Portland
Old Lobster Fisherman
202
Laconia
28
109
Biddeford
Rochester
Dover
Concord
Portsmouth
101
93
Haverhill
Salem Witch Museum
A t l a n t i c
Methuen
Lowell
128
O c e a n
Malden
Peabody
Hood Milk Bottle
Boston
Weymouth
Brockton
3
Woonsocket
6
24
Fall River
Barnstable
New Bedford

Bubba the Lobster

Found off the coast of Nantucket, Massachusetts, in 2005, this leviathan lobster was given the moniker "Bubba" after being shipped to a Pittsburgh fish market. A typical lobster weighs in at around 1 ½ pounds, but Bubba tipped the scales at a whopping 22 pounds, leading scientists to narrow Bubba's age to somewhere between 50 and 100 years. Although he was spared from the dinner table, Bubba died of a bacterial infection shortly after being donated to the Pittsburgh Zoo, which plans to use the shell in an educational display.

The Old Lobster Fisherman

Boothbay Harbor, Maine

A fitting mascot for Brown's Wharf Restaurant, Motel & Marina, this stoic, yellow-clad angler consists of wood, steel, and fiberglass and measures 25 feet from boot to cap. Operated by the Brown family since 1946, Brown's Wharf installed the big guy a quarter-century later.

THE PAPER HOUSE

Rockport, Massachusetts

BEGINNING IN 1922, Elis Stenman layered newspaper, glue, and varnish to create the walls and furnishings of his two-room house. Surprisingly, the place has withstood the test of time. Inside, you can still read the print on the newspapers that make up the desk, tables, chairs, grandfather clock, and bookshelves.

Great American Sports Destinations

- Fenway Park, Boston, Massachusetts
- Indianapolis Motor Speedway, Indianapolis, Indiana
- Baseball Hall of Fame, Cooperstown, New York
- Churchill Downs, Louisville, Kentucky
- Pebble Beach Golf Links, Pebble Beach, California
- Football Hall of Fame, Canton, Ohio
- Wrigley Field, Chicago, Illinois
- Basketball Hall of Fame, Springfield, Massachusetts
- Lambeau Field, Green Bay, Wisconsin
- Augusta National Golf Club, Augusta, Georgia

HESS
DUNKIN' LATTES
Ford
Budweiser
AVAYA
FENWAY PARK

Big Blue Bug
Providence, Rhode Island

Since 1980, this giant blue termite has been catching the attention of passing motorists from its perch atop the New England Pest Control building. The pest, named "Nibbles Woodaway," is 9 feet tall, 58 feet long, and weighs 4,000 pounds. The company even dresses Nibbles for several holidays: a white beard and patriotic top hat for the Fourth of July, a witch's hat and broom for Halloween, and a red nose and antlers for Christmas.

Eartha

Yarmouth, Maine

The world's largest rotating globe, Eartha is housed in a three-story glass atrium at the headquarters of map company DeLorme. The globe weighs nearly 6,000 pounds and has a diameter of 41 feet, 1 1/2 inches. It was designed using satellite imagery as well as more traditional mapping data to represent the planet as seen from space. Eartha rotates on a mechanical axis and is meticulously detailed, with visible cities and even roadways.

MUSEUM OF BAD ART

Dedham, Massachusetts

"CONVENIENTLY LOCATED just outside the men's room" in the basement of the Dedham Community Theater, the Museum of Bad Art presents and preserves bad art in all of its regretful glory. About 25 classic tasteless works (out of a collection of 250, many of which were salvaged from trash cans) are on display at any one time.

Green Cowboy by Martha

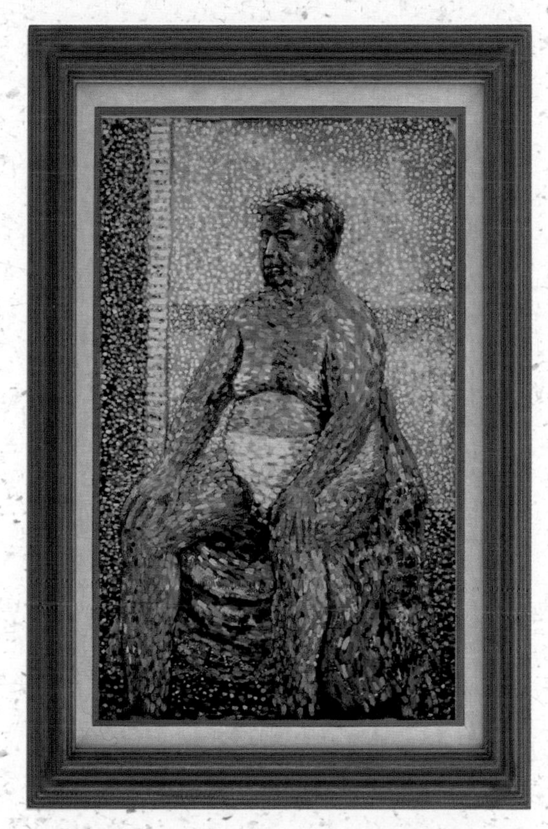

Sunday On the Pot With George by Unknown

Guarding the Rock by Unknown

Salem Witch Museum

Salem, Massachusetts

In 1692, 20 men and women were executed in Salem for the crime of practicing witchcraft. The Salem Witch Museum gives visitors a lesson in the town's history as well as a look at changing perceptions of witchcraft through the ages. Each October, ghosts and goblins (and witches) abound during the town's Haunted Happenings festival.

Hood Milk Bottle

Boston,
Massachusetts

Likely the most memorable structure on the Boston Wharf, this 40-foot milk bottle stands a stone's throw away from the site of the Boston Tea Party. While it currently houses a snack bar, it could hold about 50,000 gallons of milk if push came to shove.

THE SOUTH

THE SOUTH BECKONS WITH a sultry mystery, drawing travelers to back roads rich in both history and beauty. There's still a little feeling of being a foreigner in a strange land for outsiders who venture here, but the locals' famous hospitality gives road-trippers a reason to stay awhile. The culturally diverse region offers something for everybody: soul food and barbecue for food lovers, theme parks and beaches for the young in spirit, and music for blues and country and western fans—not to mention the Southern-fried roadside attractions that dot the highways.

Everglades National Park
Florida

GRACELAND

Memphis, Tennessee

THE HOME OF ELVIS Presley is now a prime road-trip destination, attracting visitors as both a rock landmark and the Taj Mahal of American kitsch. The King of Rock 'n' Roll bought the place in 1957 and lived there until his 1977 death. Elvis stamped each room of the mansion with his unusual taste. The jungle room houses Polynesian-inspired furnishings and has a waterfall coursing down the wall. The pool room isn't dominated by the pool table, but by the walls and ceiling, which are swathed in the loudest fabric money can buy. A visit to Graceland isn't complete without a peek at the Meditation Garden and the King's final resting place.

"I don't regard money or position as important. But I can never forget the longing to be someone. I guess if you are poor, you always think bigger and want more than those who have everything when they are born." ELVIS PRESLEY

Great American Musical Destinations

Preservation Hall,
New Orleans, Louisiana

- Graceland, Memphis, Tennessee
- Country Music Hall of Fame, Nashville, Tennessee
- Carnegie Hall, New York City, New York
- Experience Music Project, Seattle, Washington
- Buddy Holly Center, Lubbock, Texas
- Rock and Roll Hall of Fame, Cleveland, Ohio
- Delta Blues Museum, Clarksdale, Mississippi
- Motown Historical Museum, Detroit, Michigan
- CBGB, New York City, New York
- Preservation Hall, New Orleans, Louisiana

Graceland Too

Holly Springs, Mississippi

Paul McLeod may well be the world's most dedicated Elvis fan. Want proof? For starters, he named his son Elvis Presley McLeod. He also named his house after Graceland, the King's Memphis abode. Like its inspiration, Graceland Too is open for tours each day. McLeod's comprehensive Elvis collection contains thousands of records and CDs, countless pieces of memorabilia, and pictures, posters, and original art covering nearly every square inch of wall and ceiling. Tours often include a dab of Elvis impersonation for good measure.

Chair

Anniston, Alabama

An apt advertisement for Miller Furniture in downtown Anniston, this 33-foot chair trumps numerous big chairs scattered across the planet. This is one chair you don't want to lean too far back—it might flatten a brick building.

Chest of Drawers

High Point,
North Carolina

Originally known as the "Bureau of Information," High Point's big chest of drawers was constructed as a monument to the city's status as "Home Furnishings Capital of the World." The 40-foot-tall chest is actually the facade of a building—the home of the High Point Jaycees.

PASAQUAN

Buena Vista, Georgia

PASAQUAN IS THE CREATION of folk artist St. EOM, also known as Eddie Owens Martin. After returning home in 1957 from a long stint in New York City, St. EOM spent the last 30 years of life turning Pasaquan into a multihued fantasyland of artistic fusion, in between telling fortunes for those who sought out "The Wizard of Pasaquan."

PASA

The Big Chicken

Marietta, Georgia

Originally the home of a greasy spoon called Johnny Reb's, this eatery, adorned with a 56-foot-tall sheet-metal chicken, has been a Kentucky Fried Chicken location since 1974. KFC considered demolishing the place after high winds damaged the bird in 1993, but public outcry led to a complete restoration.

Jimmy Carter Peanut

Plains, Georgia

Created by Democrats in Indiana for a Jimmy Carter visit during his presidential campaign, this 13-foot peanut pays homage to the former president's peanut-farming background and toothy grin. Its creators subsequently gave it to the president, and it now sits only a stone's throw from his onetime campaign headquarters.

MYRTLE BEACH

South Carolina

ONE OF THE TRUE meccas of Southern tourism (not to mention Southern kitsch), Myrtle Beach is the crown jewel of the "Grand Strand," a 60-mile stretch of coastline bounded by the Waccamaw River and the Atlantic Ocean. Beyond the sandy beach itself, Myrtle Beach throws out bait to road-trippers in the form of two amusement parks, a bustling nightlife, and water sports galore. The Myrtle Beach area is also home to 50 miniature and more than 115 full-size golf courses, earning the title "Golf Capital of the World."

"Golf combines two favorite American pastimes: taking long walks and hitting things with a stick."
P. J. O'ROURKE, *MODERN MANNERS*

The Mississippi Delta

GREAT MUSIC, tasty vittles, and eccentric attractions line U.S. 61 through the Mississippi Delta. Dedicated road-trippers will also want to hit the UCM Museum, just across Lake Ponchartrain from the Big Easy.

Historic Voodoo Museum
New Orleans, Louisiana

Graceland
Peabody Hotel
Delta Blues Museum
UCM Museum
Preservation Hall
Historic Voodoo Museum
MISSOURI
KENTUCKY
ARKANSAS
TENNESSEE
MISSISSIPPI
ALABAMA
LOUISIANA
Gulf of Mexico
Rolla
Lebanon
Salem
Farmington
Springfield
Joplin
Houston
Ava
West Plains
Cape Girardeau
Poplar Bluff
Carbondale
Evansville
Owensboro
Lexington
Paducah
Madisonville
Bowling Green
Somerset
Hopkinsville
Clarksville
Nashville
Cookeville
Murfreesboro
Rogers
Springdale
Harrison
Paragould
Dyersburg
Jonesboro
Blytheville
Ozark National Forest
Fort Smith
Jackson
Columbia
Athens
Cleveland
Chattanooga
Russellville
Conway
Forrest City
Memphis
Savannah
Florence
Huntsville
Mena
Little Rock
Stuttgart
Decatur
Fort Payne
Rome
Hot Springs
Pine Bluff
Clarksdale
Tupelo
Gadsden
Nashville
Hope
Cleveland
Jasper
Texarkana
Greenwood
Columbus
Birmingham
Magnolia
El Dorado
Greenville
Starkville
Kosciusko
Tuscaloosa
LaGrange
Yazoo City
Ruston
Monroe
Columbus
Shreveport
Meridian
Montgomery
Vicksburg
Jackson
Troy
Natchitoches
Natchez
Brookhaven
Laurel
Many
Alexandria
Hattiesburg
Enterprise
Dothan
Thomasville
De Ridder
DeFuniak Springs
Mobile
Baton Rouge
Lafayette
Gulfport
Pensacola
Lake Charles
Panama City
New Iberia
Port Arthur
New Orleans
Houma

UCM MUSEUM
ABITA SPRINGS
OPEN
COLD
DRINKS

UCM MUSEUM

Abita Springs, Louisiana

A LABOR OF LOVE for artist John Preble, the UCM Museum (pronounced You-See-'Em Museum) is "Louisiana's most eccentric museum," and that is a serious understatement. The consummate roadside attraction features everything from the "House of Shards," bejeweled with chunks of shattered pottery, to "Aliens Trashed Our Airstream Trailer," a mobile home impaled by a flying saucer. Elsewhere, the museum houses Buford the Bassigator, collections of pocket combs and paint-by-number masterworks, a shrine to Elvis, and a miniature river town.

Gates of Gatorland

Kissimmee, Florida

While the sharp-toothed jaw of an angry alligator might not be anyone's idea of a tourist magnet, it's a fitting doorway to Gatorland, a 110-acre zoo/theme park dedicated to all things slimy and scaly. Thousands of real gators call the place home, but—while gator-wrestling competitions aren't uncommon—this is the only mouth visitors should enter.

Sharkheads

Biloxi, Mississippi

Tourists must bravely venture into the jagged, 35-foot-tall maw of an ornery great white shark if they want to walk away with the T-shirts and other souvenirs within. The beached polystyrene killer of the deep is the gateway to one of the largest souvenir/swimwear/sundry stores on the Gulf Coast.

"SEE ROCK CITY" BARNS

IN THE 1920S, GARNET CARTER ENVISIONED a residential development atop Georgia's Lookout Mountain. He built a house, and his wife built a superlative rock garden, incorporating natural formations with sculptures of all kinds. After realizing people might be willing to pay to see the latter, the couple cast out a tourist-trap lure by the name of Rock City. Next, they sent Clark Byers out to implement a unique advertising campaign: Byers would approach farmers and offer a free paint job on one side of their barns if he could add the words "See Rock City." The concept caught on quickly, but the farmers soon demanded a few dollars in addition to the free paint. There once were 900 barns emblazoned with the slogan "See Rock City" dotting the countryside from the Midwest to the Deep South, but time has not been kind to them: Fewer than 100 remain.

When You See
ROCK CITY
You See The Best

Shell-shape gas station

Winston-Salem, North Carolina

This relic is the last station standing out of eight built by Quality Oil to sell Shell gasoline. No longer an operational station, the concrete, wood, and wire structure fell into disrepair before Preservation North Carolina rescued it and converted it into a regional office.

South of the Border

Dillon, South Carolina

At the junction of three highways just south of the North Carolina–South Carolina border is one of the kitschiest spots on the East Coast. This constantly expanding mecca of Mexican-theme kitsch now includes 350 acres of shops, motel rooms, restaurants, and even an amusement park dubbed PedroLand. The neon-clad complex is centered on a 200-foot tower shaped like a sombrero, with an elevator that goes all the way to the top.

PEABODY DUCK MARCH

Memphis, Tennessee

SINCE THE 1930s, THE LUXURIOUS Peabody Hotel has served its guests impeccably, but a few lucky ducks get the best treatment of all. At 11:00 each morning, the Duck Master, clad in red and gold, escorts a quintet of mallards from the rooftop Royal Duck Palace to the marble fountain in the lobby where they spend their days. Everything is first-class: They ride down in a special ducks-only elevator and waddle down a red carpet that's laid out just for them. At 5:00 each evening, the procession is reversed, as the ducks retire to their palace for the night.

STATUE OF LIBERTY

Home: Liberty Island, New York

Created: 1886, as a gift to the United States from France

Height: 305 feet, 1 inch (ground to torch)

Made of: copper over an iron frame

Best features: The statue's crown has seven rays to represent the seven seas and continents and 25 windows that represent the gemstones of the world.

JUNK STATUE OF LIBERTY

Home: McRae, Georgia

Created: 1986, as a gift to the town from the Lions Club

Height: approximately 35 feet (ground to torch)

Made of: polystyrene, a tree stump, and other recycled materials covered in green paint

Best feature: The statue's head was carved (using a chainsaw) from a tree stump.

CORAL CASTLE

Homestead, Florida

After his beloved fiancée called off their wedding at the last minute, Ed Leedskalnin spent 28 years building an ornate castle as a monument to his lost love. Leedskalnin used only hand tools to cut the massive blocks of coral—1,100 tons in all—that form the castle walls. In between moving and carving the giant chunks of coral, Leedskalnin gave visitors tours and sold pamphlets that expressed his famously eccentric views on love, politics, and magnetic currents. Three days after leaving a note on the castle door—"Going to Hospital"—he passed away in 1951, leaving the castle to his nephew. His nephew sold the place, and the new owners found Ed's life savings soon thereafter: thirty-five $100 bills, collected a dime (and later a quarter) at a time—the price of admission.

Fountain of Youth

St. Augustine, Florida

The site of a natural spring that Spanish explorer Juan Ponce de León mistook for the legendary Fountain of Youth in 1513 is now a kitschy attraction with touristy diversions of all kinds. The spring's water is free for the taking—but you have to buy the souvenir bottle in which to take it home.

Ave Maria Grotto

Cullman, Alabama

Brother Joseph Zoettl, a Benedictine monk at the St. Bernard Abbey, spent nearly five decades painstakingly creating miniature versions of 125 renowned structures. Created from mixed media such as cement, stone, seashells, tiles, and glass balls, Zoettl's grotto includes the Roman Colosseum, a pint-size Holy Land ("Jerusalem in Miniature"), Spanish missions, and the Statue of Liberty.

MARDI GRAS

New Orleans, Louisiana

FRENCH SETTLERS IN ALABAMA may have been the first to celebrate Mardi Gras in the New World, but these days nobody throws a bigger party than the good citizens of New Orleans. The tradition began when the French flag flew over New Orleans in the 1700s, but the Spanish government that followed put the kibosh on the event. It was resurrected after the U.S. government took over in the 1820s.

The annual celebration—held the two weeks before Catholic Lent, culminating in Fat Tuesday—is the nation's biggest blowout, a spectacle that's risqué, chaotic, and over a million revelers strong. The parades are the true heart of Mardi Gras, organized by a number of "krewes" and featuring elaborate floats and the gaudiest assortment of costumes conceivable. For road-trippers who can't make it to the big party, there's a New Orleans museum—Mardi Gras World—that gives visitors a peek into the float-making process.

Happy Mardi Gras
Jean Lafitte's
OLD ABSINTHE HOUSE
SINCE 1807
DESIRE
Bourbon

Solomon's Castle

Ona, Florida

Howard Solomon is a sculptor whose primary medium is found and recycled objects. His biggest undertaking—at 10,000 square feet—is his personal residence, which he started building more than 30 years ago. With a shimmering facade of recycled printing-press plates, a tower with a bed-and-breakfast suite, and numerous galleries to showcase his unusual art, the castle was on the market at the time of this writing, with an asking price of a cool $2.5 million.

Cinderella's Castle

Orlando, Florida

Cinderella's home is located on Main Street USA in Walt Disney World. The castle was designed to replicate as nearly as possible the castle in the animated feature *Cinderella*. Mosaics along the walls inside the castle depict the story of Cinderella, and the princess herself hosts breakfast at the second-floor Royal Table Restaurant.

Peanut

Ashburn, Georgia

The brainchild of A. R. Smith, Jr., this monstrous goober is a symbol of Georgia's position as the top peanut-producing state in the union. Right in the thick of peanut country, the 20-foot fiberglass monument can be seen from I-75.

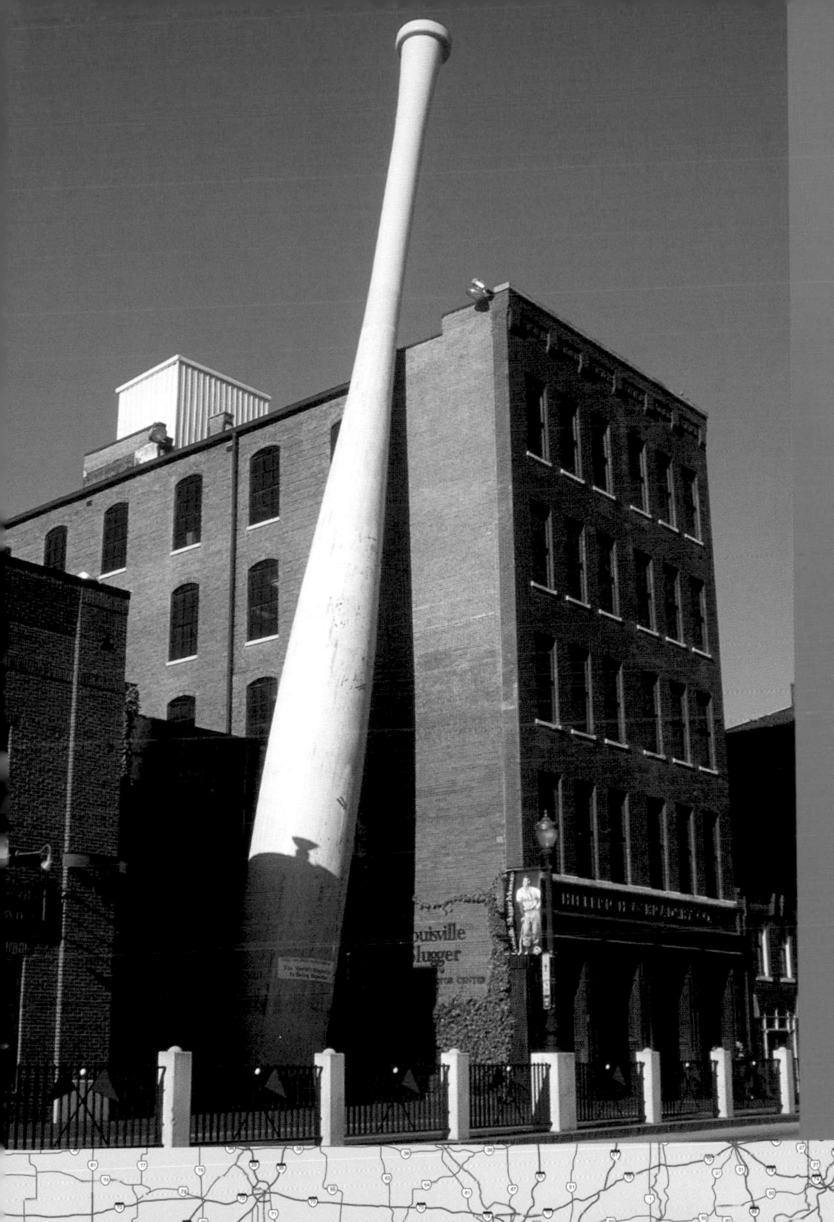

Baseball Bat

Louisville, Kentucky

Leaning against the Slugger Bat Factory and Museum is a bat that has no equal, measuring 120 feet from tip to tip and weighing in at 34 tons. The steel bat is a scale replica of Babe Ruth's 34-inch Slugger. Close at hand are the World's Largest Baseball and the World's Largest Baseball Glove.

Great Smoky Mountains National Park

North Carolina and Tennessee

ONE OF THE MOST popular national parks in the system—with over 9 million visitors a year—Great Smoky Mountains National Park is a target for road-trippers of all stripes, from RVers to hardcore hikers. Encompassing the southern Appalachian Mountains, the park's varied elevation (which ranges from 875 feet to 6,643 feet above sea level) supports every kind of forest found in the East, including 100 species of native trees. The mountains themselves are some of the world's oldest, with somewhere around 250 million candles on their birthday cake.

Gatlinburg Space Needle

Gatlinburg, Tennessee

The Great Smoky Mountains' answer to the Seattle landmark went up less than a decade after the original but never garnered the same level of fame. Featuring a 3,600-square-foot observation deck 342 feet above town, the tower is now the centerpiece of an amusement park.

Nashville Parthenon

Nashville, Tennessee

This impressive edifice was flimsily built for the Tennessee Centennial Exposition. Restored in the 1920s and again in the 1990s, it is a reminder of the Music City's reputation as the Athens of the South. Inside the majestic facade is a 42-foot-tall statue of Greek goddess Athena, said to be the largest indoor statue in the Western Hemisphere.

GEOGRAPHICAL APPENDIX

PHOTO CREDITS

Front cover: **John Elk III.**

Back cover: **John Elk III** (bottom); **PhotoDisc** (top right); **Planet Art** (top left).

Accent Alaska: Ron Niebruge, 73; **AIA Houston:** 150, 151; **Alan Clifford:** 42; **American Dime Museum:** 230, 231; **Andrea Wells Photography:** 62; **AP Wide World Photos:** Ronald Agnir, 240; John Bazemore, 284; Robert F. Bukaty, 269; Jack Dempsey, 110, 111; David Duprey, 224; Cheryl Gerber, 278; Jim McKnight, 246–247; Lisa Poole, 264–265; *San Angelo Standard–Times,* Rick Smith, 136; Cliff Schiappa, 201; Keith Srakocic, 262; *Stockton Record,* Amelita Manes, 32; Mark J. Terrill, 37; **Art Car Parade:** Harrod Blank, 154, 299; **Ben & Jerry's:** 254, 255; **Bob Young Photography:** 98–99; **Bobbi Lane Photography:** 184; **The Bomber Restaurant:** 49; **Brand X Pictures:** 28, 126, 130; **Buffalo Bill Museum and Grave, Golden, CO:** 123; **C. M. Russell Museum:** 93 (top); **CCCVB:** 216; **Colorado Gators:** Lynne Young, 129; **Coolstock.com:** Collection, 54, 310; ©2005 Olsen, 196; ©2005 Saari, 172; ©2005 Witzel, 55; **Creative Services:** Charles W. Plant, 285; **Dennis W. Finley:** 141–142; **Denver Public Library, Colorado Historical Society, and Denver Art Museum:** 93 (bottom); **John Elk III:** 34, 35, 39, 87, 106, 171, 188–189, 212; **Elwin Trump Photography:** 138; **Enchanted Highway:** 178, 179; **Fair Haven Photographs:** Joanne Pearson, 258, 263; **First State Bank of Norton, KS:** 181; **Maureen Blaney Flietner:** 204; **Folio, Inc.:** Walter Bibikow, 67, 229; Richard Cummins, 293; Jeff Greenberg, 198; **Funny Farm:** 60, 61; **Gene O'Bryan of the Loon Ethnic Arts & Craft Festival:** Barb Fivecoate, 203; **Getty Images:** 242–243, 251; AFP, 95; Allsport, Jamie Squire, 286; Hulton Archive, 50, 175, 176 (bottom), 241; David McNew, 94; Frank Micelotta, 176 (top); Scott Olson, 194; Mario Tama, 277, 279; Time Life Pictures, 71, 250; **Grace Davies Photography:** 273; **Greater Houston Convention and Visitors Bureau:** 134-135; **HCS:** Anthony Scherer, 189; **High Point CVB:** 281; **Holiday World, OH:** 211; **The House on the Rock:** 206, 207; **Houserstock, Inc.:** Dave G. Houser, 10, 103, 165, 292; **HTJ:** 70; **Mark Hundley:** 16; **Image Club:** 72 (bottom); **The Image Finders:** Howard Andre, 118; Betts Anderson, 199; Jim Baron, 209; Mark E. Gibson, 27; **Image-State:** 280; **The Image Works:** Eastcott/Momatiuk, 170; Jeff Greenberg, 291; **Index Stock Imagery, Inc.:** Walter Bibikow, 92, 104; Sally Brown, 312–313; Jim Corwin, 11, 19; Jules Cowan, 160; David Davis, 274; Ewing Galloway, 6; Mark Gibson, 210, 311; Jeff Greenberg, 105; Phil Lauro, 108; Ernest Manewal, 76, 77; Wendell Metzen, 306; Omni Photo Communications Inc., 302–303; Joseph B. Rife, 177; Jim Schwabel, 101; Stock Montage, 182; Richard Stockton, 306–307; Rudi Von Briel, 238; Amy & Chuck Wiley, Wales, 100–101, 126–127; Barry Winiker, 228; **The Integratron:** Al Kissler, 31; **Jack Olson Photography:** 65, 98, 113, 128, 168–169, 180, 197; **James Rowan Photography:** 187, 202; **Robert Kaye:** 21; **Kerouac Commemorative Memorial:** Ben Woitena, Artist, 252; **Laurence Parent Photography:** 148 (left), 162; **Longhorn Grill:** 102; **Loveland Castle:** 216–217; **Luke Cole, www.lukecole.com:** 192; **Archie McPhee:** 58; **Michael Morton Photography:** Michael Morton, 144, 145; **Al Michaud:** 200, 256, 257; **Missouri Division of Tourism:** 214; **Mount Horeb Mustard Museum:** 190, 191; **Mummer's Museum:** 243; **Museum of Bad Art:** 271 (bottom left & right); Martha (top left); **N.Y.S. Department of Economic Development 2005:** 222; **Nature Society:** 186; **New England Pest Control:** RDW Group, 268; **New Mexico Tourism Department:** 96, 97 (left); **Nichols Designs:** D. B. Cooper, 125; **Nik Wheeler Photography:** 14, 26, 36, 107, 304; **North Dakota Tourism:** 164; **Oklahoma Tourism:** Fred W. Marvel, 86; **Orange Show Center for Visionary Art:** Paul Hester, 154–155; **The Original American Kazoo Company:** 225; **Out 'n' About Treesort:** 52; **Palace of Gold:** 244, 245; **PhotoDisc:** 22, 56, 59, 66, 74, 90, 114, 142, 147, 166, 194, 215, 223, 233, 234, 259, 260, 290, 300; **Photri, Inc.:** 232; **PIL Collection:** 15, 159, 220, 276; Between the Covers Rare Books, Inc., 253; **Planet Art:** 13, 45, 69, 83, 109, 133, 161, 183, 219, 249, 275; **Randy Wells Photography:** 20; **Murray Riss:** 298; **Roadside America:** 226, 227; **Robert Holmes Photography:** 64; **Greg Ryan, Sally Beyer:** 213; **Saga Design:** Monte Sanford, 63; **Santa Claus House:** 72 (top); **Shambhala Mountain Center:** 116, 117; **Jon M. Smith:** 148 (right); **Solomon's Castle:** Jared F. Martinez, 308; **SuperStock:** 44, 46, 80, 236; Age Fotostock, 18, 24, 38, 43, 51, 82, 88, 120–121, 248, 315; Tom Algire, 132; Bill Barley, 286–287; Tom Benoit, 17, 30, 40, 41; Tom Brakefield, 97 (right), 294; Ron Brown, 218; Jeffrey Cable, 78; Culver Pictures, Inc., 163, 221; Richard Cummins, 88–89; Ron Dahlquist, 47; Raymond Forbes, 272; Max W. Hunn, 305; Ray Laskowitz, 288; Brian Lawrence, 90; Roger Allyn Lee, 79; James Lemass, 266–267; Joanna McCarthy, 131; James Urbach, 81; Edmond Van Hoorick, 68; Steve Vidler, 12, 25, 309; **The Telfair Enterprise:** Kelly M. Arnold, 301; **Texas Department of Transportation, J. Griffis Smith:** 137; **Tinkertown Museum:** 84, 85; **Tom Till Photography, Inc.:** 297; **Transcendental Graphics:** 122; **Transparencies:** Jack Harris, 296; **Wesley Treat:** 139, 146, 149, 152, 153, 157, 158–159; **Clayton Turner:** 282, 283; **UCM Museum:** 290–291; **Unicorn Stock Photos:** Deneve Feigh Bunde, 193; Jeff Greenberg, 314; Andre Jenny, 173; Mike Morris, 112; Chuck Schmeiser, 156; Jim Shippee, 119; Aneal Vohra, 174; **Uniroyal® Tire:** 208; **Voodoo Doughnut:** 48; **Jeff White:** 33; **Wisconsin Department of Transportation, RJ and Linda Miller:** 205; **©Wyoming Travel & Tourism:** 124.

GREETINGS FROM
TEXAS
TEXAS STATE FLAG
TEXAS LONGHORN

WASHINGTON

Greetings from
MEMPHIS

Greetings From
NORTH DAKOTA

hello
FROM
SOUTH DAKOTA

Greetings from
Niagara
Falls

THE GARDEN STATE

GREETINGS FROM
MAINE

Greetings from KANSAS

Greetings
from the
Aloha State
-Hawaii

WELCOME
TO
OKLAHOMA

CALIFORNIA

GREETINGS FROM
CALIFORNIA
PLAYGROUND OF THE NATION
PORTLAND
OREGON
Greetings from the Aloha State -Hawaii
WELCOME TO OKLAHOMA
UTAH
GREETINGS FROM TEXAS
TEXAS STATE FLAG
TEXAS LONGHORN
Greetings from
MINNESOTA
Greetings From NORTH DAKOTA
Greetings from KANSAS
Greetings from
NEW JERSEY
THE GARDEN STATE
GREETINGS FROM
MAINE
Greetings from
LOUISIANA
Greetings From
Florida
GREETINGS FROM
ATLANTA
Georgia
ALABAMA
Baltimore
MD.
Greetings from
BOSTON
hello
FROM SOUTH DAKOTA
Greetings from
Niagara Falls
MEMPHIS TENN.
Greetings from
PHILADELPHIA
Pa.
Greetings from
VIRGINIA
WASHINGTON